Foreword by Dr.

WHAT IS
HOLDING
YOU BACK?

IT IS TIME...

TO RECEIVE
THE BEST
GOD HAS
FOR YOUR
Life

C. E. HALL

Cover and interior design by Monica Nagy
ChristianCovers.org
Monica@ChristianCovers.org

Publishing Services provided by:
M&N Marketing Group
Printed in the United States of America

ISBN: 978-0-9966536-6-4
Library of Congress Control Number: 2019939445

First Edition: May 2019

To order your copy of *What is Holding You Back?*
Log onto: **www.KingdomLifeUSA.com**

Table of Contents

Dedication

My wife and My children and their children's children.
May this revelation of His Love and Truth be passed down
from generation to generation.

Acknowledgments

I want to honor and thank all those who grew with me and stayed faithful throughout the process of this journey.

**The Father,
The Son and the Holy Spirit**

Mom & Dad

Kingdom Life Ministries
The Staff
The Minister's of Life
The Congregation

Nick Henry

**Monica Nagy
ChristianCovers.org**

Foreword

I have known Gene Hall for about five years and have been privileged to *"sit at his feet"* and learn from the many visions and revelations he has had. The truths that he teaches in *"What's Holding You Back"* are not ethereal concepts but are rather practical explanations of why the body of Christ isn't walking in the purity and power it is destined to accomplish. His insight on how to mature into our destiny, while brilliantly conveyed, is a painful journey that he himself has lived and proven that God is faithful.

If you have never understood the depths of *"the truth that will set you free"*, this book is for you. After reading this book, I finally understood why trials were necessary in my life and why I had to *"take my thoughts captive"*. After all, Jesus is returning for a church *"without spot or wrinkle"* and many of us are still bound by the *"spots"* of unforgiveness, shame, and rejection. As my good friend and author, Jack Frost once told me, *"Hurt people, hurt people. Whole people heal people"*. Reading this book has helped me and it will help you toward wholeness.

We have believed lies for too long! These *"spots"* have been exposed by Gene and by your acceptance of this revelation of truth. You too can bring wholeness to others as you discover and fulfill your destiny!

God has used Gene Hall to show us the way to victory. I pray that he will soon have another revelation on *"wrinkles"*. Having watched Gene walk in victory for several years, I know the truth he reveals in this book will expose the lies you may have believed.

Your journey through *"What's Holding You Back?"* will be painful, but it will be worth every step of the way.

—*Lee Brandt, D. Min, Th. D., Ph. D.*

Endorsements

The truths in this book are priceless!!! After years of investing in education and working as Certified Clinical Trauma therapist, I have finally been given access to wisdom that is truly life changing. I have personally and professionally witnessed how the teachings on *"The Spots"* (Unforgiveness, Shame, and Rejection) reveal and heal the soul wounds of a person who has experienced trauma. Like an arrow to a bullseye, this book will target and allow you to pinpoint the beliefs and thoughts that prevents mental, emotional, and spiritual wellness.

Teneka G. Miles, LCSW, CCTP
Licensed Clinical Social Worker, Certified Clinical Trauma Professional
Covenant Counseling Services, LLC.

We are moving forward and no longer held back. A major testimony within our marriage begins with the teachings of this book. When we each found personal and spiritual healing by identifying our spots, we started breaking strongholds that held us back. Under the leadership of C. E. Hall, our personal growth led to professional growth as we moved into the fullness of God's love. We have been freed from shame and guilt and self rejection that had limited our life and our family for many years. Being justified in Christ, we experienced a sense of righteousness while pursuing righteousness. This strength has manifested in our business and careers as well as our roles in ministry and in our community. Together, we recommend this book, *"What is Holding You Back?"* You will find the answers in your personal self awareness that will unlock, with confidence, the next season of growth that God has for you.

Shauna Mattingly, LCSW
Cameron Mattingly, Global Account Executive, Worldwide Sales

What is holding you back is a must read. I highly recommend this book for all Preachers of the Gospel because it helps bring satisfaction to your lives by showing how to establish a relationship with God, maintain a relationship with God and nurture a relationship with God. It also provides invaluble teachings on how to glorify God by uplifting the Name Jesus' Christ and allowing the power of the Holy Spirit to rest, rule, and abide in your lives and demonstrating love for others. There is no other way to gain satisfaction and fullfilment in this life other than through complete surrender of our lives to Jesus', walking with Him and obeying His Word.

Rev Beverly G. Jordan

Introduction
Do You Feel Held Back?

What keeps you from being the man or woman God has destined you to be? What stands between you and the peace you had the day you were saved? What keeps you from loving God with all your heart, all your soul, all your strength, and your entire mind? What is that *"thing"* that haunts you and that keeps you from fully obeying the Lord? What is the secret sin that would destroy you if others discovered it's existence in your life?

There is a time in our lives when we hit a moment, or rather a crisis; a place of discovery where we identify a series of repeat performances that is ultimately set up to change our lives. A place where we know we need to redefine or find who we really are. It is accompanied with a deep desire in our heart to have a divine destiny revealed. There is a place where we all start to realize that we are not making it. We feel like we are drowning in a pool with no bottom for our feet to touch, so we can spring up for that desperate breath of air. As our feet are searching without direction for a secure place to rebound from our crisis, which is reflecting our poor choices and circumstances laced in confusion. Our arms are floundering with fear to find the surface to land a secure place of love, truth, and security. We would climb up the tallest mountain to seek and search out levels of understanding that might help us to have a clear and calm view in which to see. While in hopes to land on a solid foundation to rest our mind and soul, we never seem to find that place of understanding.

At the same time, we have become worn out mentally, physically, financially, and socially. Our spirit is shot and void of any life. Truth is a term that we take lightly due to our own ignorance of research. Truth is usually revealed to us through our connection to whatever assembly, group, or family order we are born into. Our environmental and emotional exposures to these connections impress our thoughts, activating our words, and deeds into form. From there, we perform our choices based on that seed of truth. Most of us neither question it nor apply reason to understand the movement taking place around us. We just act with a reaction that becomes what we believe *"TO BE"* the truth of our real nature. We then, in turn, believe that *"TO BE"* is the right way. *"TO BE"* is a place we create in our heart and mind that is our realized nature and truth. We own it, build it, and see it to be true, but never really experience or obtain the fullness of happiness and joy that we anticipated. Deep down, all of us are in search of an end where we are at rest; a permanent place of everlasting bliss where we enjoy all the good things life has to offer.

Disappointment takes us over, we are robbed, we find someone else to blame, and in most occasions, we do not understand why this crisis is happening to us. Our sight was blinded, the direction was unknown, and we feel like the answers are hidden from us on purpose. In our prideful elevation of self, our hearts call out and say, *"I did it the right way"*, *"That is the way I was taught"*, *"So* and so is to blame, they did not do their part correctly.", "This has to be right." After all, if it is our truth, and we believe it and it has to be right; but the evidence of the outcome isn't even close to the anticipated results.

There is an appointed time in all our lives that we realize our way is the wrong way and we feel as though we were robbed like a thief in the night. We cry out *"I need help!"* We search for a counselor, a mom, a mentor, a doctor, or a medication to show us a way to get to where we need *"TO BE"*. We've jumped over walls to gain education, climbed mountains, taken anxiety medications and do just about anything to just make things right. We are in search and seek mode to find a quick and fast answer, so we can land the ultimate love, the ultimate peace, and an ultimate joy in an ultimate place of our own PERFECTION, and have been driven by our unmet needs becoming drained of the real joys of life.

The questions emerge: What are the real joys of life? Who robbed us of our joy? How did we go the wrong way? Who did we follow? Who are we, really and where are we going in life? It all becomes a blur of confusion and a bleak future with no light at the end of the tunnel.

"Most assuredly, I say to you, he who does not enter the sheep-fold by the door, but climbs up some other way, the same is a thief and a robber. But he who enters by the door is the shepherd of the sheep. To him the doorkeeper opens, and the sheep hear his voice; and he calls his own sheep by name and leads them out. And when he brings out his own sheep, he goes before them; and the sheep follow him, for they know his voice. Yet they will by no means follow a stranger, but will flee from him, for they do not know the voice of strangers." (John 10:1-5, NKJV)

It is TIME to follow the true Sheppard! It is TIME to know His Voice!!!!

In this book you will read about three individuals; Levi, Deborah, and David and connect with their Journey of Faith to find The True Sheppard through The Doorway of Change. They, just like all of us were moving along in life doing good works that they were raised to believe, but they never obtained the fullness of those beliefs. In their minds they were seeking the promises of a happy, healthy, and secure life. They believed in a god but did not expect to receive promises from that god. Promises of a good life came from hard work, good education, special talent, or being born into the right family. All their promises were in earning a good living to support their families so that they could have bigger homes, better cars, establishing a quality in their materialistic life with enough money for retirement. They were looking to complete The American Dream that our world has caused us to believe in all its wealth and fame.

They are no different from anyone reading this book. But, in time there came a defining moment, a crisis that each one needed to find *"The Door"* that would open to *"The Truth"* of real change. They desired and hungered for *"The Truth"* to lead them through this hallway toward their destiny.

In their crisis they were being called to enter into the divine destiny that God planned for their lives. It was the moment for promotion into His Plan. YES, God has a divine plan for you, not only to obtain eternal life, but a life more abundantly. Recognizing *"The Door"* is just the start of the pure Journey of Faith in Christ Jesus so you can experience and receive the BEST God designed for your life.

"I am the door. If anyone enters by Me,

he will be saved, and will go in and out and find

pasture. ¹⁰ The thief does not come except to steal,

and to kill, and to destroy. I have come that

they may have life, and that they may have

it more abundantly." (John 10:9-10, NIV)

Shackles of the Mind

It was just past midnight as the evening service ended; people were slowly making their way toward the door. They were giving each other hugs and kisses as they headed out of the ministry toward the parking lot. A few were hesitating as the room was filled with the tangible presence of God. The place was laced with a thick cloud of God's Glory, and many were still huddled in corners and seated on the chairs within the sanctuary. It was as if they wanted to absorb the last drop of love, peace, and joy out of the atmosphere before returning to the responsibilities of their worldly lives.

Among those few are Levi, Deborah, and David. These three ministers are good friends, and the three of them love the Lord with all their hearts. They were among those who seemed less eager to depart the atmosphere of the ministry because they enjoy being in God's presence more than anything in the world. They love to worship God and they love the revelation that comes from being in His presence. They also love the company of other believers who radiate the light and life of Christ as they mutually grow to become mature in unity of the body of Christ.

The leader of this ministry, David, is the owner of a successful commercial and residential construction company. Deborah is a transplanted professional from the Northeast, who teaches in the ministry and brokers a real estate firm. Levi is a compassionate evangelist and singer in the ministry, who works in remodeling sales throughout the week. Although these three committed Christians are now enjoying a vibrant and rewarding relationship with the Lord and ministry is now the centerpiece of their lives, it was not always like that for these three friends and coworkers. Each of these followers of Christ entered the ministry in a different way and each of them walked his or her own unique path. They transitioned from a life of missing the mark to a life of service to God and people; from knowing of a God to having a relationship with the One True God; from living for the promises of the world to experiencing His Promises to them through the power of His Word.

Finding the right door and being led by the right Shepherd was the key. Each of them had to overcome struggles and destructive patterns of thinking to draw close to the Lord and to find God's destiny for their lives. Each of them has a history of wrestling with certain compelling, internal beliefs hindering them in their early pursuit of spiritual maturity and in their quest for God's will for their lives.

Since coming to the revelation of living in Christ, these three friends have now become quite familiar with His Way through the doorway of change and spending quality time every day in worship, prayer and meditation upon God's Word. They moved from religion and regulation to a revelatory relationship with the Good Shepherd. They learned to share their faith with others as well; not only in practical ways, but also through their personal testimonies of struggle in the crisis and triumph in His victory. They have grown to become His people; productive ministers working as *"one"* in the body of Christ and effective representatives of the Lord in the professional arenas where God has placed them.

In fact, since coming to Christ, Levi, Deborah, and David have experienced a lot of changes in their lives. They have ventured in their journey of faith toward spiritual maturity, becoming not only successful, but significant in the various roles that they fill, recognizing and understanding the unseen forces that used to compel their lives and the past experiences that used to govern their thinking in less than wholesome ways. Through relationship with the Lord, God has made them aware of these compelling, invisible forces that used to drive them versus the inner, impelling power of the Holy Spirit working as one with the revelatory word of God. In this process of maturity, the Lord has set them free from the strongholds that Satan's power had on them through their lack of knowledge regarding God's Word.

Many years ago, David was living in manic depression. Fear seemed to be keeping him from finding that true happiness and peaceful satisfaction that he desperately wanted for himself, although brimming with external confidence and a strong sense of self-control. Deborah felt as if she were being held back from accomplishing what she knew she could achieve with her life. Because of inner insecurities, something was hindering Levi from walking in the confidence that he needed to give full expression to his musical talents and the brilliant sense of humor that God had given him. This is the way it is with many people today—even committed Christians—who face struggles like this in their lives. Although they have traveled far in certain areas of personal growth, a lot of them seem to never make progress in other areas. Sometimes, they even regress in certain aspects of their faith and devotion.

It makes sense that an unbeliever would struggle when it comes to the unseen spiritual aspects of his life. Many unbelievers know deep within their hearts that God is real, and that God is good, even though they don't believe they are worthy of His goodness. People find it difficult to act on what they know about their

Creator, because of being consumed by its creations. They find it difficult to surrender their lives to the Lord or to draw close to Him or serve Him in any meaningful or consistent way because their *"connection"* to God is blocked, and something seems to be keeping them from surrendering their lives to Christ and trusting Him with their happiness.

What is surprising, however, is that a lot of Christians have this very same problem. They know in their hearts that God loves them, and His grace is enough response to all their spiritual needs. They also know they have the capacity to be great husbands, great wives, great parents, and great disciples. They have the capacity to do significant things for the Lord and for mankind. Yet these believers struggle, like their unbelieving counterparts, with the internal feeling that something is wrong, something is missing, or something is keeping them from the full realization of their potential as human beings and as children of God. They struggle because they cannot figure out how to obtain the abundant life in Christ or what the deficiency is in their lives.

Why can't they be more consistent in doing what they know is right? Why can't they avoid the all-too-familiar sins, moral, mental, and physical failures that seem to be a regular part of their lives? Why can't they break free from certain types of thinking? Why do they still seem drawn to friends and behaviors that they know are detrimental influences on their wellbeing? Why can't they seem to *"break out"* or become the kind of people they know they have the capacity to be?

People are trapped in an internal mental prison—just as Levi, Deborah, and David were trapped—and they don't know how to break free from their personal bondage. They are trapped, and don't know what is causing the problem that haunts them. They just know that something is wrong. Something is wrong in their hearts, something is wrong in their lives, and something is lacking in their relationship with the Lord. They would do almost anything to enjoy the kind of life they know God created for them and to be free from the invisible forces that deprive them of the inner peace that they seek.

Deep down they know something is holding them back, yet they have no idea what to do or where to turn. They don't really want to talk to anyone about their problem because the unbelievers around them don't understand spiritual things and other believers can be judgmental. Therefore, many Christians, especially those with good reputations, don't want their pastors or fellow church members to know they are having these daily struggles. Besides, they wouldn't know what to say to their pastors or their friends, even if they felt the freedom to confide in them because they are convinced that other people could never fully understand what's going on inside their hearts. For this reason, these struggling individuals just keep silent as they wrestle in their soul with the realization that something is missing from their lives. They resign themselves to the fact that this is the way life is going to be for them. This is just the way things are.

People don't realize how common these feelings can be among people both inside and outside the church. They don't realize that this problem was common among people living in the first century, as well, and on through every century. Believers and unbelievers alike have been dealing with spiritual *"strongholds"* in their lives since Eve was deceived in the Garden of Eden. They are dealing with strongholds that affect their relationship with the Lord, spilling over, having an impact on every other dimension of their lives.

STRONGHOLDS

The idea of strongholds was first introduced by the apostle Paul, who wrote to the believers in Corinth during the first century AD, telling them: *"For the weapons of our warfare are not carnal but mighty in God for pulling down strongholds, casting down arguments and every high thing that exalts itself against the knowledge of God, bringing every thought captive to the obedience of Christ, and being ready to punish all disobedience when your obedience is fulfilled." (II Corinthians 10:4-6, NKJV)*

Strongholds are really nothing more than the grips Satan has on us, the *"claims"* that he makes on certain aspects of our lives through our erroneous thinking. This is the place in our soul that we allowed the enemy to establish his throne in our lives. They are first established in the mind, which is why we are to take every thought captive. In fact, Paul told the believers in Ephesus, they should.... *"neither give place to the devil" (Ephesians 4:27, KJV), "and do not give the devil a foothold." (Ephesians 4:27, NIV)*

The word used in this statement for *"place"* and *"foothold"* is the Greek word topos, which means *"an opportunity"*, *"a region of space"*, or *"a room."* We would never willingly give the enemy a *"region of space"* or *"a room"* in our soul that he can use as a *"place"* to control the direction of our behaviors through our thinking.

It is possible, not only for unbelievers to have strongholds in their lives, but for Christians to have these strongholds as well. It is possible for God's people to yield to *"places"* in their lives to Satan. Paul, in his epistles to the churches at Corinth and Ephesus, would open his greeting *"to all the saints"*.

Paul wanted these believers to know more than merely the fact that this possibility exists; Paul wanted the members of the churches to know how Satan succeeds in his efforts to gain that place in our lives. He especially wanted the people to know that the enemy's stronghold begins in the mind as a thought. Through yielding to this thinking, we hand over our authority with agreement like a signed and sealed contract, giving our possession over to Satan in which he gains access to our souls and succeeds in controlling certain aspects of our lives. When we yield through *"arguments"* Satan claims his hold in our minds and our hearts. *"Every high thing that exalts itself up against the knowledge of God." (II Corinthians10:5, NKJV)*

THE LIE

Behind every stronghold we find a lie, a place of personal bondage where God's word has not been planted or rooted. That lie is an unscriptural idea or an inaccurate belief that is held to be truth. These lies are detrimental to the spiritual health of our soul. *"Beloved, I pray that you may prosper in all things and be in health just as your soul prospers." (III John 1:2, NKJV)*

Identifying the lie matters; when we accept the lie in our soul, we will eventually act upon it through our thoughts, words and behaviors. Our soul is the producer of our thoughts. When we act upon a thought, we build our lives around it, whether it is a lie or truth. What we accept and agree to in the soul, we become.

Why do we fall into deception? Why do we chase after ideas and fall prey to beliefs that have no basis in reality? Why do we allow Satan to grip an area of our lives by thinking about things, believing things that simply aren't true?

First, we must equate our soul as land or a territory to be owned and possessed. I call the soul the *New Testament Garden* that Jesus died for it to be reclaimed or redeemed. Second, we must identify the rooms or courts of our soul. I call these the Functions of the Soul: they are the Intellect, Will, Emotions, and Affections. These are the courts/rooms in our soul that are in constant movement.

We entertain lies because we are desperate for *"movement"* in our lives. We are desperate for forward progress. We need solutions to our problems and solid foundations upon which we can make our choices and build our lives. However, because God's truths don't always come to us quickly or effortlessly and are often hard to accept and obey, we sometimes invent our own truths to sustain ourselves temporarily or accept the truths that the people around us instill in us through conventional wisdom or tradition. However, if the *"truths"* we embrace turn out to be lies, we pay the price for believing them and for implementing them in our lives. Therefore, God warns us against such things. He loves us too much to stand silently on the sidelines while we destroy our lives and miss the mark of His purposes for us.

FEAR

Fear becomes the driving motivation behind our human tendency to accept the lies of Satan. We fear drifting through the storms of life without a paddle. We fear facing the dilemmas of life without some type of moral compass. If God's paddle isn't readily available to us, when we haven't saturated our minds with the biblical truths that apply to the situation we are facing, we simply grab the first paddle we can find, and we start rowing in the direction that seems most logical to us. Unfortunately, when we land on the wrong shore or our ship sinks during the crossing, we often blame God for the outcome, for not loving us in the way we think He should.

In the same way we tend to eat certain foods that comfort us in times of distress, we also tend to believe certain *"truths"* that comfort us in times of distress. This is how Satan succeeds in making a room in our spiritual house of the soul and claims ground within our lives—our marriages, our finances, our relationships, our sexuality.

IDOLATRY

An unknown stronghold begins with inaccurate thinking, and inaccurate thinking flows from the acceptance of a hidden lie. Likewise, all lies are conceived through blinding fear, and behind every fear is idolatry. That's right, idolatry!

When the volcano is erupting, and the natives are afraid for their lives, their fear drove them to conjure up all kinds of imaginary gods in their minds, gods who must be angry with them for some reason, gods who have the power to save them from certain death if the natives can only find a way to appease these angry gods. So, these fearful natives create images of the gods they have imagined, and they cast idols of the images they have visualized in their minds to appease these lifeless forms with animal sacrifices or some other gift or performance.

If you are tempted to think this is an irrelevant comparison, you should realize this is precisely what the Israelites did in the wilderness when Moses was not present to enforce God's laws. This is the same thing we do today when we face the challenges of life without the leadership of a mature pastor or the personal revelation of Scripture.

While Moses was on top of the mountain with the Lord, the fear that the Israelites had about their unknown future caused them to imagine all kinds of things in their minds. These vain imaginations caused them to fashion an idol of a golden calf and start worshipping it. When we find ourselves removed from the Truth of the Spirit we need during times of doubt and uncertainty, we also tend to formulate lies in our minds. The acceptance of these lies leads to fear. Fear leads to the formation of an idol in our minds. An idol lives in that room or place that God wants to possess. In fact, idols would not exist anywhere in the world if people would simply learn to trust in The Spirit of God and His Word, as well as the spiritual resources that have been made available to us through Jesus Christ.

Unfortunately, we don't always know the relevant principles of God's Word, nor have we learned to apply the principles we know to the real situations that confront us. Instead, our thinking is more influenced by the world, a world that is dominated by blinded fear and hidden vain imaginations created by these distortions of thought. Just because a person is saved doesn't mean his mind has been renewed to think accurately all the time, or that he has purged all the residue of unscriptural logic from his mind since coming to Christ.

Salvation of our Spirit, the born-again experience, is instantaneous, but sanctification of the soul is a lifelong process after we have come to Christ. The strongholds Satan has established in our souls since we were born from our mother's womb, through our ungodly thinking, or generational hand-me-downs, must be discovered and must be *"demolished"* one step at a time. *"For the weapons of our warfare are not carnal but mighty in God for pulling down strongholds." (II Corinthians 10:4, NKJV)*

Even though God won't do all the work for us, He has provided us help in this battle by arming us with the weapons we need to fight the unseen forces that affect us. He has given us the Name of Jesus, *"And these signs will accompany those who believe: In My name they will drive out demons; they will speak in new tongues;" (Mark 16:17, NIV)*

He has given us the blood of the cross, *"They triumphed over him by the blood of the Lamb and by the word of their testimony; they did not love their lives so much as to shrink from death" (Revelation 12:11, NKJV),* and He has given us His written Word to equip us for victory. *"For the word of God is alive and active. Sharper than any double-edged sword, it penetrates even to dividing soul and spirit, joints and marrow; it judges the thoughts and attitudes of the heart. ¹³ Nothing in all creation is hidden from God's sight. Everything is uncovered and laid*

bare before the eyes of him to whom we must give account;"
(Hebrews 4:12-13, NKJV)

Therefore, as these spiritual weapons are mastered and utilized, strongholds are toppled, and soul bondages are broken in our lives.

What's holding you back in your pursuit of spiritual maturity?

What keeps you from being the man or woman God has destined you to be? What stands between you and the peace you had the day you were saved? What keeps you from loving God with all your heart, all your soul, all your strength, and your entire mind? What is that *"thing"* that haunts you and keeps you from fully obeying the Lord? What is the secret sin that would destroy you if others discovered its existence in your life?

It is important to understand that your spiritual maturity, working out your salvation in Christ, has nothing to do with your initial salvation. Your eternal salvation is the instantaneous work of grace. The moment you heard the Good News and believed the Gospel, the moment you repented of your sins and confessed your faith in Jesus Christ as the risen Son of God, your spirit was saved and reconciled back to God. You can never do anything to become *"more saved"* or *"better saved"* than you are today. In fact, if you could become *"more saved,"* your salvation would become a matter of your own efforts and your own works.

On the contrary, you have become a new creature in Christ Jesus and your salvation is not a matter of your own works; it is a matter of God's work on your behalf. Your simple trust in the fact that Jesus died for you, will sanctify you and bring you forth into your spiritual maturity. When we place our trust in Jesus for the salvation of our soul that He has made available to us, our sins are forgiven, and our names are written in the Lamb's Book of Life for all eternity.

The salvation of your spirit is quite different from the salvation of your soul. Your spirit was regenerated once and for all when you confessed Jesus as your Savior and asked him to forgive your sins. When you embraced Jesus' death for you on the cross, the indwelling power of God's Holy Spirit was imparted to your spirit and you became a child of God. However, your soul is being saved little by little. Your soul is being renewed gradually by the Word of God as the Holy Spirit removes the residue of the lies you once believed and replaces those lies with the truth of God's Word. God is renewing your soul, therefore, by renewing your mind. He is transforming your life by making you Christ-like in your thinking.

This means it is possible for the people of God—people who are truly saved—to be missing out on the abundant life Christ has purchased for us. For this reason, Paul wrote to the believers of his day, encouraging them to... *"reach unity in the faith and in the knowledge of the Son of God and become mature, attaining to the whole measure of the fullness of Christ." (Ephesians 4:13, NIV)*

Paul promised believers of his day that, when they achieved this level of maturity in their lives, they would... *"no longer be infants, tossed back and forth by the waves, and blown here and there by every wind of teaching and by the cunning and craftiness of people in their deceitful scheming." (Ephesians 4:14, NIV)*

The fact that Paul encouraged this kind of growth in the Christian life tells us that it is common for the people of God—people who have experienced salvation of the Spirit—to be held back from the true riches of God's Word and to cease their spiritual progress because of their lack of knowledge. Therefore, the book of Hebrews adds to the admonition in Ephesians, encouraging us to *"move beyond the elementary teachings about Christ and be taken forward to maturity, not laying again the foundation of repentance from acts that lead to death, and of faith in God." (Hebrews 6:1, NIV)*

God wants His children to grow up and become increasingly mature in Christ (sanctification). God's children will always be His children, even when they behave in immature ways. In the same way that an earthly father wants to help his children grow in their self-reliance and practical functionality, God wants to help His children grow in spiritual wisdom and understanding. God's wisdom always flows from relationship with His Word.

Therefore, God's answer to our lack of knowledge is more of the Word, but strongholds are those unscriptural ideas in our lives that resist the truth of the Word. They are the imaginations, behaviors, habits, tendencies, and familiar ways of thinking and behaviors that govern our lives and continually make us susceptible to Satan's trickery and the deception of men. They are the internal thought mechanisms that cause us to repeatedly fall into the same familiar patterns of behavior and the same familiar traps that keep us in the cycle of repeat performances. This keeps us from attaining the whole measure of the fullness of Christ in us.

Solomon wrote, *"Desire without knowledge is not good—how much more will hasty feet miss the way!" (Proverbs 19:2, NIV)*

It is the nature of the believer to begin his Christian journey with enthusiasm, but unless that he adds knowledge to his enthusiasm, he will never grow spiritually. The Word of God is the only sufficient and reliable source of divine knowledge that we have at our disposal.

This explains why strongholds are so detrimental to our spiritual growth and development. Satan's strongholds resist the wisdom of God's Word and refuse to yield to it. When love, light, and truth come near to that protected place of fear or hurt in our lives, Satan puts up his defenses in our soul like a wall to block our ability to hear God. So, God cannot gain access to our soul's bondage, and expose the dwelling lie and remove it. We resist the unction of the Holy Spirit, our Helper and Counselor, and stubbornly hold onto those lies that are opposed to God's will and Word. The stronghold's grip will grow stronger in time and the soul bondages in our lives will grow more and more resistant to God's love, light, and truth. As a result, our souls become prisoners to the lie and our own vain thoughts start to burst out and produce that lie into an Oscar winning movie in full 3D in our mind, and we become subject to the outcome of the kingdom of darkness.

We must never forget, however, that God is not content with this. God created us to be His OWN. He redeemed us to serve Him, to follow Him, and to become increasingly like Him so we might glorify Him through our lives and impact others on His behalf. He wants to not only be our Father but our friend, also. We are empowered by the Spirit of God, the Holy Spirit working within us, to be complete and whole in Christ Jesus. We are empowered by the regenerated Spirit to be complete in our spirit, soul, and body. We are empowered to manifest this wholeness in our finances and relationships.

As I have explained, this process begins at salvation, when God saves our spirits through faith in Jesus. Jesus becomes our savior. As the Lord begins to change our souls, He surgically removes from our lives all the *"residue"* of our past experiences, past conditioning, and old ways of thinking and behaviors. As God touches these various aspects of our lives—one at a time—and we yield these areas of our lives to Him—one at the time—He changes us, moves us *"from glory to glory"*. He works to perfect His image within us. As every new revelation is embraced and applied, we become increasingly more like Him and more useful to him as trusted servants. Jesus is our Lord, the Lord of our lives.

How many Christians know what it is like to bask in the fullness of God's love, yet struggle in one or more areas of their lives? How many know what it is like to repent over and over for the same shortcomings or failures without making any progress in those areas of their lives? How many are tossed to and fro by the deception of others and by their own self-deception? How many feel *"stuck,"* asking themselves in the secret recesses of their own hearts; *"Is this all there is to the Christian life?"* How many have wandered off course from the destiny God gave when He first called them to be His own because they could not successfully overcome bondage in their lives?

If you have a place of personal bondage in your life where you think the will of God is ineffective, then you have a stronghold in your life. A stronghold is that compelling force which holds you back, that *"thing"* which keeps you from achieving victory in a specific area of your life. It is that *"place"* where Satan abuses you, controls you, and brings death and destruction to your life in some way. The existence of strongholds doesn't make any sense when we read what the Bible says about the people of God.

The apostle Paul declared in his letter to the Ephesians that Jesus will return for a bride who is without *"spot, or wrinkle, or any such thing"*.

He said that the church of Jesus Christ would be *"holy and without blemish"*. So, how do we reconcile this apparent contradiction? How do we reconcile the fact that we currently live with *"spots,"* *"blemishes,"* and *"wrinkles"* when the Bible clearly states that Jesus will return for a church that is without *"spot, wrinkle, or any such thing"*? We reconcile ourselves to this apparent discrepancy by realizing that we, within our soul, may not be free from these *"spots"* right now, but the Good News is that we have the capacity to be free from them. We have the capacity to surrender ourselves to the authority of Jesus Christ and deal with these *"spots"* by allowing them to be consumed by the fire of God's love. Through the Word, we are purified, so the strongholds of Satan can be eradicated from our lives.

At the end of the first century, the apostle John wrote to the churches, *"Let us be glad and rejoice and give honor to Him: for the marriage of the Lamb is come, and His wife hath made herself ready." (Revelation 19:7, KJV)*

How has the bride of Christ made herself ready for her wedding day? How has she prepared herself for her everlasting union with her bridegroom? She has made herself ready the same way an earthly bride would make herself ready: by removing the *"spots"* and the *"wrinkles"* and the *"stains"* that have kept her from walking in the purity the Lord requires. She has kept herself *"unspotted from the world"*. Where she failed to keep herself unspotted, she *"overcame"* the things that formerly defiled her. *(James 1:27; Revelation 2:7, 11, 17, 26; Revelation 3:5, 12, 21)*

In this book, I want to help you understand some of the *"spots"* and *"blemishes"* that contaminate our soul and keep us from being the type of people God has destined us to be. I want to expose some of the strongholds that Satan creates in our lives, some of the footholds that he establishes to manipulate us. I want to help you understand that *"spots"* are the leftovers, the *"residue"* of deception in our souls. They are the natural consequence of the fall of Adam and Eve in the Garden of Eden. These *"spots"* can create targets that Satan uses to attack our lives. They create the opportunity where he gains a foothold in our souls. I also want to show you how you can be free from these *"spots"* and *"blemishes"* by learning to apply the Word of God to those areas that remain undeveloped or spiritually dysfunctional in your life.

Levi, Deborah, and David are good examples of people walking out their salvation and moving forward from glory to glory. They are born again and know God in a personal and intimate way that impacts every aspect of their daily existence. Remember, it wasn't always this way. At different points in each of their lives, Levi, Deborah, and David struggled with the spiritual strongholds that hindered them from experiencing the full power of the Gospel and hampered them in their pursuit of spiritual maturity. Like every individual with spiritual strongholds, you will discover how Levi, Deborah, and David couldn't see what was happening beneath the surface in their own hearts. They couldn't understand the unknown, hidden, and blind forces that were controlling their every thought and deed.

In chapters four, five and six I will be sharing with you the personal stories of these three real-life individuals and the experiences that each of them had in their struggle against the invisible forces that controlled them. They had vain imaginations that influenced their thinking, ultimately producing a bad circumstance. I will also share with you the truth about how they came to understand what was holding them back and how God, in His true nature and divine power, freed them from the tightfisted grip of sin and the principalities of darkness. I will share how the Lord performed the miracle of salvation in each of their lives and how He redeemed them through the awareness of His grace toward the salvation of their souls. First in their spirits, removing the *"wrinkles"*; and finally in their souls, cleansing the *"spots"* so they can be liberated to mature in Christ.

Our *"spots"* are places where God can do the greatest work of deliverance in our lives. Our *"spots"* are places where God can show us His grace and the true manifestation of His glory. This is where we learn to let God's Word purify our souls the way His Son has purified our spirits. They are the places where the truth of the Spirit and God's Word can take dominion over the lies that so readily control us. Most of all, the *"spots"* upon our souls are those places where God can change us forever because they are the places where the most significant spiritual battles are fought and won.

The Residue of Deception

The Bible clearly predicts the blessed hope of the return of Jesus Christ. According to Scripture, the day is approaching when Christ will return to catch away his bride and to usher in a series of events that will lead to the establishment of His kingdom on earth. When the Father determines that the time is right for His Son to return for the bride, *"that He might present her to Himself a glorious church, not having spot or wrinkle or any such thing, but that she should be holy and without blemish." (Ephesians 5:27, NKJV)* He will return for a church that is *"holy"* and without *"spot"*.

As it stands today, many of the believers who make up the church are individuals who are infected with *"spots."* These *"spots"* have become the places from which Satan controls our lives. They have become the spiritual strongholds from which Satan forces upon us the laws of his own kingdom, so he can thwart God's destiny for our lives.

The good news is that God has a remedy for these *"spots,"* just as He has a remedy for every other physical, spiritual, emotional, relational, and financial ailment that plagues mankind. The sobering news is that the individual believer must do the hard work necessary to rid himself of the *"spots"* that stain his soul. The church has work to do before she can say that she has *"made herself ready"* for the coming of the Lord.

All Christians have *"spots"* in their lives that demand attention, *"spots"* that need the cleansing touch of the Lord. These *"spots"* affect us more than we might know. We don't always recognize their presence in our lives or their operation because they operate behind the scenes and out of sight. Nevertheless, they are engrained in us due to our familiarity with them and our comfort with their influence. So, the task for any sincere believer is to expose himself to the Word of God. The light of divine truth will reveal the hidden things of darkness in our hearts, making it possible for God to rid us of these concealed flaws and to heal the wounds that our sins create.

"Spots" can affect us in multi-faceted ways until we understand them and deal with their presence in our lives. They can keep us from breaking out and achieving our optimum potential in God's kingdom. They can cause us to look spiritually awake when we are sleep-walking through life, because *"spots"* anchor us to the world and make us susceptible to Satan's devices. Through the lust of the flesh, the lust of the eyes, and the pride of life, the enemy of our souls can use these *"spots"* to put a *"hook"* in our mouths and use it to lead us where we do not want to go by compelling us to do things that we know we should not do.

"Spots" are those places where Satan seeks to regain dominion in our lives following the regenerating work of salvation. They are the bull's eye for the fiery darts of the enemy because Satan is not stupid. ***"Above all, taking the shield of faith with which, you will be able to quench all the fiery darts of the wicked one." (Ephesians 6:16, NKJV)***

He is smart and strategic. He knows that his attacks against us must be targeted toward our vulnerabilities instead of our strengths and must be calculated to impact us at an obvious point of weakness.

Consequently, *"spots"* give Satan a specific claim to us, a foothold or a license, as it were, to do his bidding and to frustrate God's work in a specific area of our lives. The tragedy with this, is when Satan has a claim to any portion of our lives or when we delegate authority to him in a specific dimension of our souls, he brings misery and a lack of fulfillment to every aspect of our existence. The man who is financially honest, for instance, may have no temptations in areas involving his money. On the other hand, if he struggles with sexual bondages or unbridled anger, he will never be able to fully enjoy the prosperity that God gives him. He will never be able to fulfill his calling as a husband, a father, or a leader in the body of Christ. ***"This persuasion does not come from Him who calls you. A little leaven leavens the whole lump." (Galatians 5:8-9, NKJV)***

If Satan can gain a stronghold in our lives through one or two areas that are misaligned with God's Word, he can frustrate us in our efforts to achieve God's purposes in the world and he can exercise dominion over us, though we belong to the Lord.

"Spots" are the residue of deception, the devices through which the deceiver attaches himself to us. When we give Satan, through these *"spots"*, the power that was stripped from him at the resurrection, we make ourselves subservient to his cause. We become susceptible to the lies that he tells us about God, about ourselves, about life, and about the people who are integral to our lives.

Therefore, the Word of God is so vital to the believer. God's Word is the cleansing agent the Holy Spirit wants to use to wash these *"spots"* from our lives, and the application of God's Word is the effective treatment the Lord wants to employ to heal these places in our souls. Unfortunately, if we lack enough knowledge of the Word, we are destined to struggle with these *"spots"* all our lives. If we lack the ability or the will to apply what we have learned from the Word, we are destined to revisit the truths God wants us to grasp until we come to understand the tactics of the enemy and come to the place where we can be free from Satan's control and manipulative power of our own flesh.

"Spots" cause us to perform for men and not for God, because we instinctively do whatever is necessary to conceal our weaknesses from those who would disapprove of them. We unconsciously live double lives to accommodate our *"spots"* and conceal them. We are afraid of the humiliation we might face should our friends and fellow believers learn about the attitudes and behaviors that remain unsanctified by God's Word.

"Spots" keep us from experiencing the presence that God wants us to enjoy and the future that he wants us to inherit. Instead of basking in God's goodness, we struggle with our own weaknesses and with feelings of guilt and condemnation that often accompany them. Instead of expecting the abundant life that God has promised to us as His children, we learn to fear the long-term consequences of the hidden things that drive our actions.

Therefore, *"spots"* continually toss us to and fro. ***"We should no longer be children tossed to and fro and carried about with every wind of doctrine, by the trickery of men, in the cunning craftiness of deceitful plotting." (Ephesians 4:14, NKJV) "Let him ask in faith with no doubting for he who doubts is like a wave of the sea driven and tossed by the wind." (James 1:6, NKJV)***

They keep us in unstable circumstances, where we cannot put down roots or produce spiritual fruit, where we cannot build our lives upon the solid rock of biblical truth and divine wisdom. While *"spots"* contaminate our lives, we will always be lacking in something (though we may not always know what it is). We will not be able to attain the spiritual rest that we were designed to enjoy in Christ Jesus.

"For we who have believed do enter that rest, as He said: "So I swore in my wrath, they shall not enter my rest," although

the works were finished from the foundation of the world."
(Hebrews 4:3, NKJV)

In addition to keeping us in bondage and depleting our spiritual and moral fortitude, *"spots"* also open doors to the wrong kinds of people, attracting them toward us and inviting them into the inner recesses of our lives. Birds of a feather flock together, as they say. The presence of unknown *"spots"* creates a spiritual void that draws counterfeit men and women and inevitably connects them to us, in business, love, and friendships. Our *"spots"* can cause us to attract people who have ulterior motives and people who are driven by values that are sinister in nature, because *"like calls to like"*. People eventually settle into relationships that make them feel at home and in associations that make them feel comfortable.

Consequently, *"spots"* will invite abusive people into our lives. These abusers will be wearing different masks and appear with different faces than the users who preceded them. If our *"spots"* persist, the same relationship problems will continue to inflict us as destructive people enter our lives to wreak havoc and to do their disparaging work. It is wise to remember that people are drawn to us for a reason. Relationships don't just happen by accident. If phony and abusive people seem to constantly migrate toward us, taking advantage of us in some way, it is probably because something invisible is drawing these people toward us and giving them the subconscious impression that we are vulnerable and there for the taking.

In our relationships and in the conduct of our lives, *"spots"* also feed off the power of the soulish man, particularly the emotions, thus making us reactive rather than proactive. Instead of being appropriately responsive, to the unpleasant things that happen around us, we tend to be oversensitive and volatile. Instead of dealing with disagreeable people out of a regenerated spirit with expressions of love, joy, and patience, we overreact to people with improper manifestations of the flesh, like hatred, anger.

Most importantly, *"spots"* keep us orbiting around them. In the same way that the planets orbit around the sun, never breaking ranks with the centerpiece of their existence and the controlling force behind all their movements, we instinctively and unwittingly build our lives around our *"spots."* We protect our *"spots,"* we hide them, nurture them, and strengthen them through repeated use. We excuse them, accept them, harbor them, and *"feed"* them with our time and our money. We can even ignore our health, relationships, and our own mental wellbeing in subconscious efforts to give these *"spots"* a superior place in our lives.

Sooner or later, all human beings must come into agreement with some vision or belief system that is bigger and more enduring than themselves. If we come into agreement with the Lord through his Word, our *"spots"* will diminish, fade away, and heal because the Word of God is a comprehensive remedy for everything that plagues the human soul. If we repeatedly come into agreement with the enemy through our static thinking and the behaviors that follow, our *"spots"* will remain and increase in strength and endurance. *"Spots"* on the human soul are those places of disconnect from the available grace of God.

Unfortunately, these *"spots"* exist in all of us. Until we attain spiritual perfection on the day of the resurrection, we must be attentively employed in the ceaseless battle against these powerful devices. We must constantly allow the Word of God to search our hearts *(see Psalm 139:23)* and to shed light upon our minds *(see Psalm 119:105)* so we can locate and identify these *"stains"* and allow the Holy Spirit to do within our souls what he has already done within our spirits.

Therefore, don't let God's presence in your life fool you. Don't let the anointing of God upon your life lure you into thinking that you have somehow "arrived" when it comes to spiritual maturity. *"Spots"* must always be the focus of our spiritual warfare the same way that enemy soldiers must always be the focus of a military sentry. Until the day we leave our earthly bodies and enter heaven, the *"spots"* and *"blemishes"* that are apart of the human condition will continue their deceptive work as they *"feast"* with us and affect us *(see II Peter 2:13)*.

Whether we are talking about the *"spots"* in our own lives or the *"spots"* that manifest themselves through others in the church, we must always be vigilant and maintain a watchful eye for their existence and their influence. One of the most accurate ways we can identify the presence of *"spots"* in our midst is by paying attention to the spirits that typically surround them.

Although I cannot see a fire, I still recognize the fire's existence by the smell of the smoke that accompanies it. While I cannot see my wife, I can still recognize her presence in our house by the fragrance of her perfume or the aroma of the food she is cooking in the kitchen. Similarly, though I do not have eyes that see the invisible forces at work in my own life or within the lives of others who have the power to influence me, I can still detect the presence of destructive *"spots"* by noting the existence of those spirits that accompany them.

Writing about *"spots"* in the church, Jude said, ***"they feast with you without fear." (Jude 1:12, ESV)*** Jude also said that we can recognize their presence: ***"Woe to them! For they have gone the way of Cain, have run greedily in the error od Balaam for profit, and perished in the rebellion of Korah." (Jude 1:11, NKJV)***

The spirits that accompany these *"spots"* in the church are the spirit of Balaam (which is greed) and the spirit of Korah (which is rebellion). Where we find an attitude of rebellion or greed, we find *"spots."* They are threatening to the church, to the individuals and the families that fellowship with it. Therefore, we can always recognize *"spots"* in others and ourselves by the defenses that accompany their *"spots."*

According to Jude, the people who have *"spots"* on their souls: ***"These are grumblers, complainers, walking according to their own lusts; and they mouth great swelling words, flattering people to gain advantage." (Jude 1:16, NKJV)***

This is how we can recognize such people in our midst and recognize such influences in our own hearts. By looking at the *"fruit"* that our hidden blemishes produce, we can know the true condition of our own souls and the hidden motivations of others. According to Jesus, nothing is more revealing about a tree than the fruit that it bears *(see Matthew 7:16)*, and nothing is more revealing about a man's heart than the track record he produces through his attitudes, his words, and his deeds.

Your spirit man has been washed, and it is full of the light of the Holy Spirit. That is why you hunger for God. That is why, like Levi, Deborah, and David, you love to experience the presence of the Lord. That is why you refuse to abandon God, even when you are discouraged. That is why you love the company of other Christians and why the Word of God and songs of praise move you to tears and tug upon your heartstrings.

While your spirit is washed and full of light, your soul has not been thoroughly washed. It is still groping through the darkness to find its way to the Lord. The present state of your soul is largely determined by the *"spots"* in your life, the leftovers of deception that have impacted your thinking throughout your life. The only hope for your soul, therefore, is to be renewed the same way that your spirit has been renewed. God's strategy for renewing the soul is quite different from his strategy for renewing the spirit.

The spirit, as I have explained, is renewed instantly by a confession of faith in Christ and by repentance from one's sins. When a person accepts Jesus into his heart, the Holy Spirit enters that person's life and revives his spirit instantly. The spirit of a regenerated man never needs to be regenerated any further.

However, the soul is renewed, not by an instantaneous act of grace, but rather by the lifelong process of sanctification. A person's soul is renewed as God incrementally alters his thinking through the influence of Scripture or instantaneously changes his perceptions through sudden bursts of revelation. Paul said, *"Be transformed by the renewing of your mind." (Romans 12:2, NKJV)* So, as a man's thinking is changed by the Word of God and by the Holy Spirit's enlightenment of the Word, that man's attitudes are changed, and his behaviors are changed as a result. When his life in this world is changed, his earthly destiny is changed, as well. So, the Spirit saves the spirit, but the Word saves the soul. Eternal life is realized in the spirit man, but the abundant life that Jesus promised us in this world is realized in the soulish part of a man as he allows God to change his life by changing his thinking.

One of the reasons people have difficulty with the Bible is because they fail to understand the distinction between God's promises for eternity and God's promises for the *"here and now."* They have difficulty distinguishing between those portions of Scripture that deal with Heaven and those that pertain to our earthly lives, but Jesus spoke about both. He wants us to have *"life,"* and life *"more abundantly" (John 10:10, KJV).* In other words, Jesus wants us to have eternal life through salvation, but He wants the experience of salvation to spill over and affect our thinking, so we could be changed and equipped to live a different kind of life in this world, a more fruitful and rewarding life. He wants us to be happy, healthy, and to prosper both materially and professionally. He wants our families to be strong. He wants us to create a more enduring legacy for our decendants. He wants us to have all things.

In a perfect world, the people of God should be whole in their spirit, soul, body, and their finances. In an ideal world, the people of God should lack nothing because God has promised us everything through Christ Jesus. He has promised us everything in Heaven, and everything in this life that physical creation is designed to provide.

In the real world, however, most of us enjoy certain aspects of God's provision because we have received revelation and understanding about the specific promises pertaining to those dimensions of our lives. In other areas, we fall short of God's bounty because we lack revelation and understanding in those areas of concern. The Word of God has not yet done its full work in those parts of our lives because the Word of God has not yet saturated our thinking and changed our behaviors in those areas of our existence.

In the natural world where you and I live, a man may enjoy physical health because of his level of understanding regarding God's promises about his own body. The same man may struggle financially because of his incomplete grasp of God's promises concerning prosperity and abundance. As he grows in his understanding of God's Word, however, that man will change his thinking. His changed thinking will lead to changed behavior, which God can use as a springboard for implementing the rest of his promises in that man's life. Changed thinking leads to different actions, and different actions lead to a different outcome.

Revelation is God's love chasing you down. Revelation is God opening your mind, so you can finally *"see"* what has been true all the time. A revelation of God's truth can only come through

God's Word. The Holy Spirit, who is living within your spirit, takes the Word of God and illuminates your mind with it until the light comes on inside your head and you can see clearly what you could not see before. Revelation is God's portal to transformed thinking and a transformed life. Revelation demands your cooperation to result in change because God cannot change anything that you refuse to let him change. So, revelation puts a demand on repentance. You must learn to repent, and change your way of thinking, if you want to see God change your behaviors, your habits, and the overall direction of your life.

What is a disciple? Jesus appointed twelve specially chosen men to be his disciples. In a similar sense, He has called all of us to be his disciples as well. A disciple is nothing more than *"a learner under discipline."* When the disciples first came to Jesus, they had a surface knowledge of God's Word. Their concept of God and their understanding of divine truth went only as far as their Jewish traditions would allow them to go.

Even though Jesus accepted these men immediately and loved them unconditionally, it took the Lord every minute of every day of His earthly life to change the thinking of these simple fishermen and tax collectors. He poured His wisdom into them and spent time alone with them. He taught them things that He could not teach the masses. He allowed them to witness things that others were not permitted to see. They followed Him and observed Him in difficult situations. They walked and talked with Him before and after His crucifixion and resurrection.

What made these men His *"disciples"* was the fact that they were receiving God's Word in heavy, concentrated doses. They were receiving the Word of God through His teaching, and they were receiving the Word by listening to Jesus as He interacted with others. They were receiving the Word through the stories that Jesus told about real life, and they were receiving the Word through the personal applications of truth that Jesus manifested to them individually. Peter, James, John and Matthew were Jesus' disciples because they were gradually being changed by the Word of God. In fact, they were being changed from the day they met Jesus on the dusty roads of Judea until the day they departed this world through physical death. They never stopped growing or changing because they never stopped learning the truths of God's Word.

When we start following the example of these men by allowing the Word of God to take root in our hearts, we will become Jesus' disciples the same way they became Jesus' disciples. We will grow and change because the Word of God will inject us with new truth and infuse us with new revelation. The Holy Spirit will give us wonderful *"ah-ha"* moments when knowledge from the Scriptures connects with our souls and the spiritual light comes on inside our minds. These revelations help us to grasp the concepts God wanted us to know and understand how to apply those newly acquired concepts to our lives. Then, we will produce spiritual fruit in those areas impacted by that newly obtained knowledge. We will walk in power and authority and overcome the destructive forces that have controlled our lives thus far.

Jesus told the twelve men who followed him, *"By this my Father is glorified, that you bear much fruit; so you will be my disciples." (John 15:8, NKJV)* A genuine disciple bears spiritual fruit in his life, but to bear spiritual fruit, a person must be inundated with the Word of God. To bear spiritual fruit, a person must be impacted, affected, and changed by the revelation of Scripture. Discipleship is no more complicated than receiving a steady diet of the Word of God and living out the things that you learn as God reveals those things to you. It means living out God's Word during your trials, persecutions, temptations, and even in the good times when you can easily become complacent. To *"live out"* the Word of God, you must receive and experience it to understand it.

When Paul was writing to the Ephesians about the Lord's plans to come back for a bride that *is "without spot or wrinkle or any such thing." (Ephesians 5:27, NKJV)* Paul told the believers in Ephesus that it was the responsibility of the church, that is us, to make herself ready for the day of the Lord. Then, Paul gave the believers a clue regarding exactly *how* they should begin to make themselves ready. He said that we should allow the Lord to cleanse us *"by the washing with water through the word." (Ephesians 5:26, NKJV)*

Knowledge—*Revelatory knowledge from the Word of God*—is the key to spiritual growth and maturity. It is the key to understanding what is holding us back in our efforts to pursue the Lord as disciples. It is the key to producing spiritual fruit in our lives. The Word of God, applied to our hearts by the Holy Spirit, must wash the *"spots"* that contaminate our souls. It must make us ready for the day when we will meet the Lord in the heavenlies. It must set us apart from all the people around us and clearly distinguish us as followers of Jesus. It must shine life and truth and love into our souls to eradicate the presence and power of those sins that so easily beset us.

The Word of God is *"sharper than any two-edged sword." (Hebrews 4:12, ESV)* If we don't embrace that penetrating aspect of the Word or don't allow the Word to do its work in our lives by *"cutting"* us in places where it hurts, we will never grow because we never knew the truth. We will struggle to overcome our faults and failures because we never understood the source of their strength and power. By allowing God's Word to do its work in our lives, exposing the *"spots"* that contaminate us from within, we take the first step toward freedom and wholeness. By allowing the Word of God to do its work in our lives, surgically removing the *"spots"* and *"blemishes"* that become visible in the light of God's truth, we become as clean in our souls as we are in our spirits. We become the men and women that God created us to be, and we become ready for that day when *"the marriage of the Lamb has come." (Revelation 19:7, ESV)*

What are the specific *"spots"* that hold us in bondage? What are the particular *"stains"* that give Satan a place from which to control our lives and stymie our growth? The Bible makes it clear that there are certain struggles that are common to all of God's people, and the Lord made these common struggles obvious to me through three powerful visions. Let me share with you these visions that I received from the Lord that helped me understand the nature of the most common *"spots"*. These *"spots"* keep God's people from attaining the destiny He has purposed for their lives. The *"blemishes"* keep the church from attaining the purity the Lord requires of her. If we can understand the tactics of the enemy in our vulnerabilities and weaknesses, we can resist the pull of sin upon our lives and stand against the demonic tactics that so predictably defeat us. We can uproot the flag that Satan has planted in the soil of our souls and reclaim the inheritance God has given to us as His children.

A Vision of Demonic Trickery

(View Vision on Page 62)

The Christian life is a lot like the journey the Israelites took through the wilderness when they traveled from Egypt to the Promised Land. In fact, most theologians agree that there are countless similarities between that 40-year trek and Christian life.

Like the Christian life, the journey through the wilderness began with a mighty deliverance. God rescued his people from slavery and from bondage in Egypt by performing a series of miracles that enabled them to escape their captors and begin the long march toward a special place he had promised to them through their ancestors. This is parallel to the deliverance that God performs in the lives of all who trust in Jesus. He saves us from our sin and works miracles necessary to help us escape the powers, bonds, and influences that have held us captive all our lives.

As soon as the Israelites crossed the Red Sea, they discovered an unpleasant reality that many Christians also discover once they turn away from the world and turn toward God. The Israelites discovered that there were a lot of problems standing between God's promise and God's provision for their lives.

Oh, how we love the promises of God. We can quote them all day long. We have them plastered all over our refrigerator doors and automobile bumpers. We wear t-shirts that proudly affirm them. We recite them and sing about them every time we gather for worship on Sundays. The promises of God excite and sustain us. They bring joy to our hearts and purpose to our lives.

What we never seem to consider is the same thing the Israelites failed to consider until they finally crossed the Red Sea and gazed over the eastern horizon toward Canaan. As the freed slaves stood there on the shore of the sea, watching the lifeless bodies of Egyptian soldiers washing up on the beaches of the sea's eastern shoreline, the people of God undoubtedly turned to look at the desert that lay in front them. Doing so, they probably understood for the first time that deliverance is not the final act of God's great drama in our lives. Deliverance is merely the first step in a long journey. Can you imagine how frightening that realization must have been for them because there was a lot of sand, scorpions, and buzzards standing between them and the land of promise.

Much like the Jews of old, Christians today also fail to think about the journey that is necessary to get from *"the elementary teachings about Christ" (Hebrews 6:1, NKJV)* to the promises God made to us as His people. Christians today often focus on the experience of salvation, while they forget about the struggles, they must endure to take hold of the promises that await us after salvation. The struggles are as much a part of the journey as the experience of salvation itself.

In God's time, every one of his promises will bring provision to our lives. Between the promise and the provision, we will have problems. Lots of problems! We will encounter temptation, per-secution, rejection, conflict, suffering, injustice, and hard choices. Jesus said it as clearly and concisely as anybody could say it when he told his disciples, *"here on earth you will have many trials and sorrows." (John 16:33, NLT)* The wilderness standing between God's promise and God's provision is a land of constant challenges, a place that is designed to sift us completely. We are destined as the children of God to travel through this parched land on our long journey toward the promises God has given to us.

The key to success in the wilderness is found in the way we choose to deal with the problems that our harsh environment sets before us. We can choose to be bitter or to be better because of our experiences. The same desert sun that can harden clay is also capable of melting butter. It is up to us whether we will let the difficulties of life make us harder or make us softer, make us bitter or make us better.

Unfortunately, the Israelites (all but two of them) chose to let the problems associated with their journey make them bitter. They chose to bicker and complain and thus harden their own hearts while they were making their circuitous trek toward the Promised Land. As we see throughout the account of this notable excursion, the people of God often grumbled against the Lord and often criticized their leaders because they failed to understand what God was trying to do in their midst. They failed to understand the lessons God wanted to teach them about himself and about a covenant relationship with him. They failed to take advantage of the knowledge that God was trying to convey to them through their various experiences and challenges in the harsh environment of their temporary home.

Many Christians have been miraculously delivered from bondage to the world and their own fleshly appetites seem to be on a spiritual merry-go-round, constantly revisiting the places of testing in their lives, yet never fully grasping the lessons that God wants them to learn because of their experiences. Like the Israelites in the wilderness, they gripe and complain because they cannot understand why the Lord makes things so hard for them. They cannot figure out why there is no water, why there is no food, why they must struggle just to survive, and why there are so many obstacles between them and their goals. They cannot put their fingers on the reason why they seem to be traveling in circles, never realizing the promises that God has made to them. *"Is this all there is to the Christian life?"* they ask in the secret recesses of their own hearts, never realizing that the problem is within their own souls.

In 2011, the Lord gave me a vision that helped me understand this apparent contradiction between the promises of God and the real-life experiences of God's people. More precisely, the Lord gave me three visions, and these visions enabled me to finally make sense of the dilemma that confronted the Israelites in the wilderness, the same dilemma that mystifies many Christians today.

How can God save us so mightily and with such tremendous demonstrations of his divine power only to seemingly abandon us in the wilderness? How can the Lord part the sea for us and destroy our enemies before our very eyes, only to leave us to deal with an endless array of challenges that seem to repeatedly deter us from His promises? Like the Israelites in the wilderness, why do we sometimes feel like we would rather turn around and go back to the bonds of slavery. The Bible says, *"Where there is no vision, the people perish." (Proverbs 29:18, KJV)* Where there is no vision, the people are left to struggle on their own with unanswered questions, and they usually struggle to reach the wrong conclusions. So, I asked the Lord to help me reach the right conclusions for myself and for the people he had placed under my spiritual care. While the Israelites never had such a vision or such an understanding of God's purposes in their lives, the Lord graciously gave me a vision that helped me understand His purposes and comprehend His ways. I wanted to know the full meaning of my vision, so I might not perish in the wilderness of doubt and uncertainty or lead my *"flock"* in the wrong direction through the problems of life.

I received these visions one day after two or three hours of intense worship. In my vision (artistically depicted on the pages that follow), I saw a throne, situated high atop a great pedestal. Upon the throne, there sat a black humanlike figure who was seated in front of a dark object resembling a large sphere. At the base of the pedestal, there was another sphere—a golden, glowing sphere—that was obviously the source of some type of great, life-giving power. And to the right and left of the pedestal, there was a brilliant, radiating light that illuminated the throne and several sharp objects protruding from the two sides of the throne's pedestal.

Now, I don't have these types of visions every day, so I really wanted to make sense of all the imagery and hear the voice of God amid my experience. For that reason, I asked the Lord to show me the meaning of the vision He had given to me. In response to my prayer, the Holy Spirit began showing me what these various images meant and I wrote down what He was saying to me.

The black silhouette in the vision was representative of the *"strongman."* The throne, where the strongman was seated, represented his power and authority in our lives. The dark object behind the strongman had arrows shooting out of it, so the Lord showed me that this spherical image was indicative of the *"spots"* that contaminate the souls of God's people while the arrows represented the thoughts that give rise to these spots, strengthening them and sustaining them in our lives.

The bright, glowing sphere at the base of the pedestal represented the regenerated spirit of man, the source of all light and power within the believer's life *(see Ephesians 1:3-7)*. Between the radiant image of the spirit and the dark, colorless tints of the pedestal, there was a heavy, black border, which represented the residue of the fall of man (the principle of inherited sin operating in our lives). This residue was keeping the life and the power of God within the spirit from influencing the soul of man (the pedestal), as well.

God reminded me that a man's soul consists of his intellect, will, emotions, and affections. He reminded me that the soul is the unregenerated part of man, where sin still controls us and where Satan gains access to our lives through our thinking. The soul is the place where the *"life force"* within a man's spirit finds its physical expressions in that man's life. It is the place where Satan tries to hinder the flow of God's light and life within the spirit from infiltrating the man's mind, will, emotions, and affections. It also is the place where Satan tries to reestablish his authority in the man's life following the devil's loss of that authority at the resurrection of Christ.

In the vision, there were several sharp objects protruding from the two sides of the pedestal, and stout roots were anchoring these arrows deep within the soul. The Holy Spirit showed me that these arrows were ***"the fiery darts of the wicked" (Ephesians 6:16, KJV)***, the invisible weapons that Satan uses to protect his stake in a person's soul. The *"roots"* demonstrated that demonic weapons always find their nourishment and source from within the human soul.

When the vision first appeared to me, there were six of these arrows jutting from the sides of the pedestal, and the arrows represented anger, envy, jealousy, bitterness, pride, and complaining, the most common manifestations of the stronghold of unforgiveness in the soul of the man or woman of God. The Lord revealed to me through these images that unforgiveness is one of the most common and debilitating strongholds that Satan can establish in the life of a believer. This stronghold primarily expresses itself in these six ways through the thoughts, attitudes, words, and behaviors of the person who follows Christ. The Lord showed me that the stronghold of unforgiveness and its six *"fiery darts"* were also responsible for keeping many hungry, searching souls from the ability of surrendering their lives to Christ.

As I gazed upon this amazing sight, two additional arrows emerged from the pedestal (the human soul), and it was obvious that God was showing me a second vision regarding another stronghold in the believers' life, this time the stronghold of shame. Shame, like unforgiveness, is a common and powerful weapon that Satan uses to bring bondage to the lives of God's people and to keep receptive souls trapped in their bondages. The stronghold of shame expresses itself through a total of eight *"soulish"* attitudes and behaviors: rebellion, pride, control, cursing, deception, masking, self-centeredness, and an unhealthy obsession with money.

Then I saw a third vision, this time the stronghold of rejection. The stronghold of rejection is manifested through the six expressions of sexual immorality, man pleasing, materialism, distrust, fear, and manipulation.

The manifestations of sin were different, therefore, in each of the three visions. The stronghold was different, as well. But the thing that was common in all three of these images was the dark figure seated above the stronghold that was binding the soul of the believer and the *"spot"* that always served as the backdrop to the strongman's throne. So, this strongman can take on different forms in different people's lives, and the *"spots"* can be different for different people, as well. But the objective of the strongman is the same in every situation: to establish *"spots"* that will contaminate our lives and then to bring us under the control of these *"spots"* through inappropriate thinking and emotions.

Like the Israelites, therefore, the church of Jesus Christ is still wandering aimlessly through the wilderness, wrestling constantly with the lure of bondages that were part of our former life. Because of this, we are not experiencing the abundant life that Jesus wants us to experience. We are not realizing the promises of God that the Bible puts forth as our inheritance.

We should know, therefore, that judgment is coming. Just as judgment eventually came to the Israelites in the wilderness, all of whom died before they realized God's promise to them (except for Joshua and Caleb), so judgment is coming to those of us who are contaminated with the "spots", *"wrinkles"*, and *"blemishes"* that the Bible declares unfit for the bride of Christ. But this judgment, unlike the judgment of the Israelites, will not be a judgment of sin. It will not be a judgment of vengeance and punishment, because Christ took our punishment for sin when he died upon the cross. Instead, this judgment will be a judgment that exposes the *"spots"* in our lives and then cleanses and purifies those *"spots"* so they can no longer dictate our behaviors. Therefore, this judgment will be a merciful judgment that will set us free from the forces that are holding us back.

As a Christian, the two best days of your life should be the day you were born and the day you discovered why you were born. But the *"spots"* that reside in your soul can keep you from fully achieving the purpose for which God created you. The residue of sin that is manifested through the *"spots"* which drive your unwanted behaviors can cause you to be detached from your personal destiny and out of touch with the assignment God has given to you in the work of his kingdom. What's more, the *"spots"* that govern your soul and give place to Satan are generally hidden from your view. Because you are unaware of them and unaware of their origins and what they are doing to you under the cover of darkness, you cannot be liberated from these terrible *"stains"* until God reveals them to you, judges them in your life, and purges them from your soul.

But how does God intend to reveal your hidden *"spots"* to you? How can you hope to see what you have not been able to see before? ***"The Word of God is a lamp for your feet and a light for your path." (Psalm 119:105, NKJV) "The Word of God is a*** *sharp two-edged sword that is able to divide between your soul and spirit, your joints and marrow, discerning the very thoughts and intents of your heart." (Hebrews 4:12, NKJV)* The Word of God is the instrument that the Lord employs to expose these *"blemishes"* in your life and purge these imperfections from your soul.

According to the writer of Hebrews, God disciplines His children in three distinct ways. He chastens them, rebukes them, and scourges them. To chasten a child is to discipline or punish that child, especially by restraining the child's behaviors through the introduction of consequences. To rebuke a child is to express sharp disapproval for the child's misbehavior. To scourge a child is to inject reasonable suffering into that child's life so he or she can learn a valuable lesson that cannot be learned any other way.

The Lord will use all these disciplinary tactics to save us from a greater catastrophe. He will use the correcting work of the Holy Spirit to bring us to repentance. He will use the stinging critique of his written Word to alter our thinking. He will use the sufferings that life can brutally force upon us to wash the *"spots"* and the *"stains"* from our souls that are detaching us from His promises and separating us from the abundant life that He wants us to enjoy as His children.

God would rather allow things to hurt us temporarily, so we can learn and grow from our experiences than He would to answer all our prayers for help in times of distress, because, by rescuing us from every discomfort or pain, the Lord abandons us to spiritual infancy. But God would prefer the path of discipline for His children because God is interested in our eternal wellbeing more than our comfort; He is interested in our purity and preparedness more than our temporary happiness. God is interested in transforming our minds, so He can transform our lives, and He is interested in transforming our lives, so He can change the outcome of our lives. The God who made us before sin intruded upon His world to thwart His plans for our lives is now interested in remaking us in the image of his Son, Christ Jesus.

However, we must cooperate with the Holy Spirit as He works to purge the *"stains"* from our souls. We must cooperate with the Lord as He does His purifying and empowering work in our hearts and minds. The grace of God cannot be manifested in your life or mine apart from the willful acts of a righteous God, but God will not act to set us free until we give Him permission to do so.

In the chapters that follow, I will share with you the revelation that I came to understand because of the visions God revealed to me in worship on that life-changing day. These visions will impart to you the things that God showed me that day about His plan to liberate us from Satan's snare and to equip us to pass quickly through the wilderness to the land of promise. Since we are the temple of God this vision reveals how God's judgments are vengeance for the enemy, but judgments of mercy for us. They are designed to cast out the intruder from the temple. God's mercy will take us to spiritual places we have never been before as we *"cast down"* the dominance of the strongman in our lives and remove the *"spots"* from our souls that so easily attract the residue of sin.

The Unknown Spot
Unforgiveness

L evi grew up in church. In fact, Levi attended a Pentecostal church during most of his teenage years, and he continued to worship at a Pentecostal church well into his adult life. Despite Levi's commitment to the Lord, his life was still marked with a lot of pain and personal tragedy.

When Levi was just two years old, his parents got a divorce, and that experience disrupted Levi's naive expectations of life. Because of his constant exposure to the scriptures, Levi thought that life was supposed to be glorious and pain free and his family was supposed live perpetually in a state of suspended bliss. Regardless of Levi's expectations, his family fell apart. As time passed, both his father and his mother remarried, forcing Levi to live in a house with a new father figure. Levi's stepmother—his father's new wife—suffered from bipolar disorder, something Levi was not prepared to handle.

Levi's life was turned upside down long before he had the emotional maturity to deal with it. In addition, Levi had to script a completely new role for himself in his new, blended family. Not only was his mother married to someone other than Levi's natural father, but Levi's mother and her new husband added two children of their own to the mix, a boy and a girl, making Levi a big half-brother to two smaller half-siblings.

All the changes in his family, the pain and challenges associated with his parents' divorce and their subsequent remarriages, caused Levi to develop a lot of anger and bitterness. Levi's helplessness in the face of all these unwanted changes caused him to become quite resentful. Over time, hidden rage grew in Levi's young heart, a rage that followed him into adulthood, invisibly contaminating his soul with deep-rooted unforgiveness. This *"hidden"* problem led to a whole new set of difficulties in Levi's adult life. Long after leaving the challenging environment of his childhood home, Levi became proud and jealous, following in his parents' footsteps by getting a divorce from his wife of ten years. This painful experience only added to Levi's anger problem and to the grip of unforgiveness upon his life.

Nevertheless, Levi was a Christian, and God was not going to allow His child to remain in this condition forever. When the right time came for the Lord to start dealing with the *"spot"* of unforgiveness in Levi's life, the Holy Spirit led Levi to a church service where I was teaching one night about the vision the Lord had given me in 2011. In the service that evening, I had all my charts and diagrams on pedestals across the stage, so I could refer to them as I taught the congregation. Levi sat there, glued to every word as he listened to me describe the devastating consequences of living one's life with unforgiveness.

Unforgiveness is the *"hidden spot,"* and it was the first of the soulish stains that God helped me understand in the vision He gave me that day. On this specific Saturday evening when Levi came to our church, I was sharing all the biblical teachings about unforgiveness that God had shown to me, as well as explaining all the insights God had helped me grasp about the destructive work of unforgiveness in the believer's life. I was also describing in detail the six *"defenses"* that Satan typically uses to safeguard his stronghold of unforgiveness in the believer's life. I was sharing personal stories and testimonies about the power of unforgiveness and its unseen function in the lives of God's people.

As church concluded that evening and people were making their way out of the sanctuary, Levi came up to me, and he jokingly commented about the six defenses that Satan employs to safeguard his influence over us through unforgiveness—anger, bitterness, envy, pride, jealousy, and constant complaining.

"I have all that stuff," Levi said with a smile on his face. Then he shook my hand and left for the night.

Levi couldn't get the teaching or the details of my vision out of his head. For the next several days, he did a lot of thinking. He thought about the way he felt victimized as a child and the way his life changed suddenly, without his consent. He thought about how much he changed dramatically over the years because of these unwanted experiences and how it affected him as an adult. He thought a lot about his failure to see what happened because it happened so slowly, so silently, and behind the closed doors of his complex and complicated personality.

Levi was born again. He believed in Jesus, and he trusted in the Lord for his salvation. He also trusted in the Lord for his day-to-day existence; but just couldn't get his salvation *"up and running."* His life was stagnant in a lot of ways, including spiritually. Levi realized that something was terribly wrong, even though he couldn't quite put his finger on the source of the problem. Perhaps unforgiveness really was part of his difficulty, as I had suggested on Saturday evening.

After all, other Christians seemed to be happier. To Levi, other Christians seemed to have a more rewarding relationship with the Lord, and their lives seemed to be marked with more spiritual depth and power. Something was holding Levi back from his full potential as a Christian, but he couldn't quite figure out what it was until that teaching on unforgiveness started helping him connect the dots and started transforming his mind to think about himself in a different way.

Levi was just *"mad"* all the time. He was easily angered and easily frustrated. Though he probably would never have admitted it, he was still angry with his ex-wife. He was still angry with his father and his mother, too. His bitterness extended to his stepmother and stepfather, who were imperfect replacements for his natural parents. He was also furious at himself. Levi's anger had woven a tangled web of undisciplined and destructive emotions in his life that were so much a part of his personality, that he couldn't even see his family's existence in his own heart.

Levi complained all the time, even about little things. In addition, he was filled with rage, a kind of rage that manifested itself even in his everyday behaviors like driving. He was still jealous toward his ex-wife, who abandoned him and rejected him. He was still angry at God and even at himself. Levi was a prideful man, deeply disappointed by the behaviors of those he trusted and deeply scarred by the false expectation that God would never allow bad things to happen to him. Even though he loved the Lord with all his heart, it was terribly stained and negatively altered by all the unseen forces that had shaped him over the years.

When he ventured into our church and listened to the teaching regarding the *"spot"* of unforgiveness and saw the charts that listed the typical manifestations of unforgiveness in a person's life, Levi was stunned. He was also convicted because, for the first time, he realized why he struggled all those years to find the joy and peace that always seemed to elude him. He realized why he approached life, and the key people in his life, the way he did. Levi's unforgiveness was distorting the way he viewed God and the way that he approached the Lord and related to Him.

Levi knew he was saved, and he knew he had a unique destiny in God's kingdom. Even when he was discouraged, Levi could look at himself and see the hand of God upon his life. He could see the many talents God had given to him for music, humor, and memorizing scripture. Even though he could appreciate these godly graces in his life, Levi could not effectively apply to his life the words he was memorizing or the lyrics he was singing. Levi's destiny was stuck in neutral, which in many ways, was worse to him than having no destiny at all.

As a born-again believer, you have a wonderful destiny in Christ. Similar to the way Levi's anger and unforgiveness stood between him and his destiny as a child of God, there may be something standing between you and the destiny God has for you. That *"something"* may be the same stronghold of unforgiveness that negatively affected Levi's spiritual growth, adversely affecting his quality of life and his future legacy as a man of God.

The *"strongman"* will always seek to distract and deter you from your destiny. The *"strongman"* will always seek to hinder you, obstruct you, and impede your progress as you try to fulfill your destiny in the work of the Lord. The *"strongman,"* the prophet of Satan, does destructive work in our lives by influencing our thoughts, attitudes, and behaviors with the *"residue"* of the fall of man *(the principle of inherent sin)*, a residue that often manifests itself through unforgiveness.

The strongman of unforgiveness is one of the *"prophets"* who represent Satan, who speak on Satan's behalf by influencing the thoughts and feelings that govern our lives. Remember, a *"prophet"* is merely one who speaks for another. A prophet of God, for instance, speaks for God and represents God to those who will heed His Words. A prophet of Satan speaks for Satan and represents Satan to those who will listen to him and allow themselves to be deceived by his tactics.

A prophet is always motivated by a specific *"spirit,"* the driving force that compels him to do what he does and to say what he says. While the prophet of God is motivated by the Holy Spirit, speaking words of truth and life, the prophet of Satan is motivated by the spirit of Balaam *(greed)* or the spirit of Korah *(rebellion)*, speaking words of deception and death to lead us away from God's life. So, each of the *"spots"* that contaminate our lives are governed and reinforced by either greed, rebellion, or both. The *"strongman"* rules over these *"spots"* and seeks to deter us from the promises of God and our destiny. He knows that these tactics are effective because the people of God are generally uninformed when it comes to Satan's strategies and to God's weaponry for pulling down the enemy's strongholds.

No matter what *"spots"* may be in our lives, the strongman, who governs those *"spots"* and utilizes them to distract us from God's will is capable of securing the foothold he has established in our souls. He is fully armed to strengthen his foothold so that his goods *(his claim upon our lives and his stake in the outcome of our lives)* can be at peace. According to Jesus, *"When a strong man, fully armed, guards his own house, his possessions are safe." (Luke 11:21, NKJV)* The strongman, who sits on the throne of authority in our lives, is both equipped and determined to maintain what he has won and to build upon the work he has established. He does this by nurturing the demonic patterns of thinking that he forged in our minds by the aftermath of life's most harrowing experiences.

Think for a moment by applying this concept to your own life. Levi's heart was changed. His thinking was altered by his parents' divorce, by growing up in an undesirable family environment, and by living through his own divorce later in life. This gave the enemy a foothold in Levi's life by causing a *"root of bitterness" (Hebrews 12:15, NLT)* to grow in Levi's soul. Levi's thoughts about God, people, life, and himself were altered by the traumatic things he experienced as a child and as an adult. Each negative experience built upon another to shape Levi's thoughts into a tangled web of angry frustration and utter disappointment.

Levi is not alone in this dilemma because the most common *"spot"* in the lives of God's people is the *"spot"* of unforgiveness. The *"strongman,"* who works to maintain an attitude of unforgiveness in people's lives, moves through the self-centered patterns of thinking imbedded in our minds. Personal offenses and patterns of thinking tend to strengthen in the presence of self-pity and defeatism. Like mold, this kind of thinking grows unabated in the warm, moist environment of a wounded heart and eventually begins to express itself in the self-destructive behaviors that follow.

Satan knows how to secure the territory gained in our souls through the introduction of unforgiving thoughts. Utilizing six devious *"defenses,"* he manipulates us the same way that a puppeteer manipulates a marionette on a string. Whenever someone gets too close to us with the truth that can help us break free from Satan's prison of unforgiveness, the *"strongman"* simply turns up the heat, so we can close our hearts and minds to the truth trying to infiltrate the protected turf within.

What are these weapons, these defenses that Satan employs to maintain a subconscious attitude of unforgiveness in our lives? The strongman employs anger, envy, jealousy, bitterness, and pride. He promotes a mindset of complaining. Through these distorted methods of viewing others and ourselves, Satan maintains a grip on our lives by nurturing an attitude of unforgiveness within us. This separates us from the blessings of God and deters us from the destiny God has established for us. When someone or something comes to us with the truth, it causes us to recognize the source of our spiritual deficiency. Then, the prophet of Satan places us in situations or circumstances, where memories of our past and emotions attached to those experiences can arouse the anger, envy, jealousy, bitterness, pride, and the attitude of complaining. This is how Satan keeps us in bondage. The strongman's *"goods"* are protected. They are *"at peace"* due to the *"fiery darts"* that Satan employs to defend his position in our lives and ward off any outside influences that might expose this *"spot"* or cause us to deal with it so we will be ready for the coming of the Lord.

What are Satan's *"goods"*? What is he trying to protect to secure his authority in our lives? The strongman's *"goods"*, for those who suffer from the stain of unforgiveness, is the inability or unwillingness of people to forgive others for offenses committed against them. Unforgiveness is the residue of the fall of Adam in their lives. It is the *"stain"* that inhibits people from discovering their untapped potential and their God-given reason for being in the world.

Remember, the spirit of a regenerated man is that place where the light of God's Spirit resides and where the truth of God's Word abides. The soul is the place where the regenerated man still waits to be renewed. So, while forgiveness is present in the spirit of every believer, the residue of the fall of man *(the principle of sin)* can keep us from manifesting forgiveness in any genuine or heartfelt way.

The spirit of man is the invisible part of a man, but the soul of man is where his spirit finds its expression. The soul is the seat of the intellect, the center of the will and choice, the headquarters of emotion, and the capital of all affection. The soul of man is that part of man that gives expression in the physical world to the unseen things that reside in his spirit. But while the spirit is filled with the forgiveness of God because it is directed by the Spirit of God, the soul can still be dominated by unforgiveness due to the residue of sin. This hinders the life of God within man's spirit from affecting his soul as well.

Therefore, the apostle Paul said that you must ***"work out your salvation with fear and trembling." (Philippians 2:12, NKJV)*** You must *"work out"* the things that God has engrafted into your spirit, so they can find their physical expression in your soul. Forgiveness must be worked out of your spirit into your soul if it is to become something more than a theological concept in your life. The only way this can happen is by changing the way you think. The mind is the link between the spirit and the soul, between confessed beliefs and resulting actions. Renewed thinking, therefore, is the mechanism that God uses to wash the soul from Satan's influences. The Word of God is the cleansing agent that God employs to renew your thinking.

Never forget that Satan's kingdom is a kingdom that is maintained by *"defensive"* weaponry, not *"offensive"* weaponry. Satan cannot take from you, by force, what God has given to you by grace because ***"no weapon that is formed against you will prosper."*** *(Isaiah 54:17, NASB)* But, Satan can certainly safeguard and protect the *"goods"* that have been bestowed upon him due to our own willful disobedience to God's laws or our own ignorant neglect of God's precepts. Satan can certainly maintain a grip on our lives through the untreated residue of sin in our souls.

We know that Satan's weaponry is defensive in nature and not offensive, because Jesus told his disciples about the future triumph of His church against the kingdom of darkness, the Lord said, ***"I will build my church; and the gates of hell shall not prevail against it."*** *(Matthew 16:18, KJV)* But *"gates,"* as you know, are defensive weapons, not offensive weapons. *"Gates"* cannot advance the position of any army or any king. However, they can certainly help a strongman solidify his position. *"Gates"* can enable a kingdom to maintain its geographical presence and ward off intruders trying to plunder the *"goods"* within the city. Satan's kingdom has *"gates,"* but his offensive weapons are useless against the child of God.

The strongman keeps us shackled with unforgiveness by erecting *"gates"* to keep the Word of God within our spirits from infiltrating our minds and emotions as well. The strongman fortifies his *"spot"* of unforgiveness in our lives by protecting, nurturing, advancing, and reinforcing it through personal offenses like divorce, abuse, and through individual trespasses like slander, deceit, or outright betrayal.

You know what it's like in your own life. You know that you should forgive people because God has forgiven you. You know you should release people from their indebtedness to you. You've read your bible and know that Jesus linked the Father's willingness to forgive you directly to your willingness to forgive others *(see Matthew 6:15)*. In your spirit, therefore, you feel like you have forgiven people for the things they have done to hurt you. You feel like you have reached the place in your life where you can forgive future sins committed against you because you understand the eternal principle that unforgiveness hurts you more than it hurts the other person. But, when those real-life opportunities come along to forgive others for their offenses, you find it more difficult than you imagined rendering the forgiveness you should. Your emotions go wild and memories of past experiences flare up when forgiveness is required. Your sense of justice overwhelms your commitment to mercy. The strongman succeeds in holding his ground and protecting his turf. His *"goods"* are preserved, and his title deed to this specific claim on your soul is secured for another day.

If you are saved and destined for heaven, why does Satan bother to do the work that is needed to maintain the *"spot"* he has secured in your soul? Why does he orchestrate so many bad experiences in your life to keep you trapped in a bottomless pit of unforgiveness? The archenemy of your soul goes to all this trouble because he is interested in keeping you from attaining the destiny that God has designed for your life. He wants to make you ineffective. He wants to cripple you and put you on the sidelines, so you cannot interfere with his agenda for the world. Satan wants to take the fire out of your belly and the passion out of your life because he knows that your life has potential to do more harm to his little kingdom than you could ever imagine. He knows your potential better than you do, and doesn't want you to achieve your destiny in life. He doesn't want you to be conformed to the likeness of Christ, and he doesn't want you to fully understand who you are in the Lord and why you are here.

The *"spot"* of unforgiveness, if not confronted, can blind us to our own value and our own potential. It can keep a person from discovering his unique reason-for-being. This *"spot"* is Satan's *"title deed"* to our lives. It is his *"license"* to control us, his *"badge of authority"* to manipulate us, and his *"right"* to bring pressure upon our lives so we will remain under his dominion in unforgiveness. It is the place of influence—his claim upon our souls—from which he limits our potential, guides our lives in a direction that God does not want us to go, directs us toward behaviors that are detrimental to our wellbeing. It is the root of his deception in our hearts.

King Solomon, who is known universally as a man of abundant wisdom, said, *"People who conceal their sins will not prosper." (Proverbs 28:13, NLT)* Our *"spots"* conceal our sins, not from God, but from us. Because we don't recognize the presence of unforgiveness within our lives, Satan maintains a foothold in our souls and a firm grip upon our thinking. Until the *"spot"* is discovered and removed, we won't prosper or reach our goals. We won't achieve that *"thing"* for which we were created. We won't identify or fulfill the purpose for which we were designed.

Fortunately, there is hope. Jesus said, *"When a strong man, fully armed, guards his own house, his possessions are safe. But when someone stronger attacks and overpowers him, he takes away the armor in which the man trusted and divides up his plunder." (Luke 11:21-22, NKJV)* So, Jesus wanted us to know that the strongman is indeed strong. While he is intent upon guarding what belongs to him and maintaining his investment in our lives, the Lord is stronger. The Lord can overwhelm the strongman's defenses and plunder the strongman's domain. The Jesus who saved your spirit is the same Jesus who can bring salvation to your soul. He is the Son of God, who has both the power and authority to take from the strongman what has been claimed in our lives through deception.

Satan, if left unchallenged, is indeed strong. He is a formidable foe whose strength far exceeds the strength of any human being. In the Bible, he is described as the opponent of God's people. He is depicted as a hater, an accuser, an adversary, an enemy, a resistor, an obstructer, a hinderer, a withstander, a tormentor, a deceiver, and a liar. He is everything that God isn't, and he isn't anything that God is. In fact, we could rightly think of him as the "anti-God," because he is opposed to God and to everything that God is doing in the world and in your life. He wants to keep God from fulfilling His purpose for your life by building a barrier between the light and life of God that resides in your spirit and the practical expression of those holy things through your soul.

He does this by establishing a *"spot"* of unforgiveness in your soul that you are unable to see within yourself. Just as a man is incapable of seeing a spot on the back of his own head, so you are unable to see the *"spot"* of unforgiveness that has been growing silently in your soul since the day Satan gained his foothold there through the offenses that caused you to stumble. Jesus wants you to know that He is capable, through His Word, of releasing the power of God in your life and plundering the house of the strongman, while destroying the *"goods"* of unforgiveness. He can expose the *"spot"* and cleanse it. He can change you. This is the good news you didn't understand the day you surrendered your life to Christ.

Remember, there are six *"defenses"* that Satan employs to guard his house of unforgiveness and to keep his goods safe. He employs anger, which is a deep feeling of displeasure often expressed through rage. He employs envy, the hidden covetousness of the soul that prompts us to desire that which we do not have. He uses jealousy, the ungrounded and excessive fear of losing another person's affection. He uses bitterness, a strong and lingering sense of animosity. He utilizes pride, a conceited, exalted opinion of oneself that leads to self-centeredness and an unrealistic sense of self-sufficiency. He utilizes an attitude of complaining, the verbal expression of dissatisfaction that results from feelings of being incomplete and dissatisfied with one's life or the things affecting it.

The most critical thing to remember as we recognize the *"spot"* of unforgiveness at work in our lives is that certain things *"trigger"* these six defense mechanisms of Satan. No nation places its military on high alert, unless there is a pending attack on that nation which is substantial and verifiable. Similarly, Satan does not employ his clever defenses, unless something with the power to overthrow him comes too close to the territory he wants to protect. Satan's only way to keep us *"minimized"* and ineffective is to keep us under his thumb. When something gets too close to the *"spot"* he has established, he becomes fearful of losing control, and he goes on the defensive.

Truth triggers Satan's defenses. Nothing can prompt a person to take inventory of his life or begin the process of change more quickly than a cold, hard dose of truth, especially biblical truth. So, when truth gets too close and a person begins to see that he has a problem with unforgiveness, Satan will inject something into that person's life to arouse anger or a sense of jealousy. The person surrenders to the emotions of the soul familiar to him, and sinks back into his old behaviors of unforgiveness, assuming it is useless to try to change and convinces himself he is simply made the way he is.

Words of life also trigger Satan's defenses. Words have power, and they impart either *"life"* or *"death."* Few words are neutral in their influence. So, when words of *"life"* impact the captive's soul—words that impart life-changing truths, inspiring promises, or positive words of encouragement—Satan distracts his victim from these words and thrusts the victim back into habits of unforgiveness.

When truth is spoken—spiritual truth—salvation is near. This activates Satan's defenses. We learn that Satan is working to maintain his grip upon our lives because whenever spiritual truth confronts us, thoughts come to us that cause us to remember why we are angry or why we have been harboring unforgiveness in our hearts. Then, words that flow from an unforgiving heart will begin to flow from our lips as well, reinforcing the feelings of bitterness and offense that we feel deep within.

When a revelation of truth or another viable threat to Satan's dominion comes too close to your life, the strongman will cause something to happen to stir your emotions. As you react out of your emotions to start complaining or expressing anger in physical ways, you will know that the enemy is defending his territory in your life and that his *"license"* to dominate you remains in full effect.

The strongman's defenses may take on different shapes and expressions. Some may be verbal, and others may be emotional. Some may be physical, and others may be mostly indiscernible. All defenses have the same purpose. They are designed to protect Satan's *"goods"* of unforgiveness. They are crafted to keep us in bondage to his devices through old patterns of thinking that never change.

Always remember this: The strongman cannot activate his defensive weapons without your permission. He cannot force you to be angry against your will. He cannot compel you to be jealous if you refuse to do so. God will not violate your will either. God will not force you to forgive others or release the offenses of the past. He will not force you to be free from shackles you have grown accustomed to wearing.

Victory and defeat boil down to a simple decision. Once the truth of God's Word enables you to recognize the source of your problem and allows you to understand God's pathway out of the darkness, it's a simple matter of agreement. You must choose whether you will agree with God or agree with your captor. You must realize that your power to choose is the combination to the lock that seals your fate. You can be free if you understand what is happening to you spiritually, but not if you are blind to Satan's devices. You can be free if you choose to let God's Word correct your thinking about unforgiveness and affect the way you approach this problem in the future, but not if you continue in your old ways of thinking, feeling, and behaving.

It begins with a thought. In fact, everything begins with a thought. When we have a destructive thought—a thought of anger, of jealousy, of envy, or of complaint—and we come into agreement with that thought by speaking it with our mouths or acting upon it in the physical world, the potency of that choice is released and the power of sin in our lives is strengthened.

The opposite is true, as well: When we come into agreement with what God has said about forgiveness in His Word and when we speak God's Word instead of our own words, then act upon the confessions we have made, another kind of power—liberating power—beings to flow through our souls and the *"spot"* begins to dissipate. The *"spot"* grows weaker as we starve it and feed the spirit instead of the carnal nature.

Therefore, the lack of knowledge of the truth or our own unwillingness to accept the truth keeps us in captivity. We come into agreement with things that we know. If Satan's *"defenses"* (anger, bitterness, etc.) are all we know, that is what we agree with. That is what we confess. That is what we embrace and act upon, and the kingdom of darkness is strengthened in our lives. If we begin to embrace the things God said about forgiveness and unforgiveness, we will align ourselves to a different way of responding to the external stimuli. The kingdom of light and life will begin to rule in our hearts.

After hearing the teaching on the *"spot"* of unforgiveness and becoming aware of his own defenses, Levi began attending more regularly. He has become a fixture in our church and in my life. In fact, he has become a good friend and a business associate.

I watched the Lord perform a miracle of restoration in Levi's life. Where he was once angry, Levi is now gentle and more self-controlled. Where he once was bitter, he has come to understand that some unpleasant things have happened to him and that he can choose whether those experiences will make him wiser or grumpier. Where he once was given to constant complaining, he is now devoted to constant praise, walking in an *"attitude of gratitude"* almost all the time. Where he once was filled with excessive pride, he has been humbled. God turned Levi's life around and set him free from a prison that had him trapped, unable to use his musical talents and his warm sense of humor to do the things that God had created him to do in the church and in the business world.

Levi was able to forgive his mother and father. He was able to forgive his ex-wife. More importantly, Levi was able to forgive himself and even forgive God, whom he blamed for all the bad things that happened to him in life. Finally, where he used to be talented at *"memorizing"* the Word, now Levi is becoming adept at practically applying the Word of God to the needs in his life. Levi has identified the *"spot"* that used to contaminate him, and he is learning to work out his salvation by replacing carnal behaviors with Godly ones.

If you tend to experience the same thoughts and attitudes over and over, and you tend to repeat the same unrighteous behaviors every time something unpleasant or challenging occurs in your life, you know why you are doing what you are doing. Now you know why you can't seem to break free to reach the spiritual maturity that is your rightful inheritance since the day you came to Christ. The truth will set you free.

Like you and me, Levi is far from perfect. He still has a lot of growing to do when it comes to spiritual things. Don't we all? The good news—the news that really counts—is that Levi has been transformed in a powerful way. He has been changed by the Word of God. He has also been healed, not only in his soul, but also in his body, because Levi's inner turmoil was manifesting itself through chronic back pain and other physical ailments that were not typical for his age. Now, this once insecure person is out of his invisible prison and free from physical pain. Levi is on his way to spiritual wholeness. He is happier than he has ever been, and he is reconnected to the God he loves.

Jesus said something very profound while he was talking to his disciples about John the Baptist. He said, ***"From the days of John the Baptist until now the kingdom of heaven has suffered violence, and the violent take it by force." (Matthew 11:12, ESV)*** This statement has many applications and addresses many issues in the Christian life, but the real motivation of this statement is that Christian life is about warfare. The Christian life is not for the weak and timid and is not for the negligent and indecisive.

To overcome the power of Satan—a power that mere humans could never fully comprehend—we must rely on the Word of God, on the blood of the cross, and on the Name of Jesus. We also must become serious about the warfare we are waging by becoming active participants in our own rescue. We must choose what we believe and believe what we choose. We must get radical and stop the advance of Satan's kingdom and its dominance over our lives and our destiny. We must release the Kingdom of God within ourselves by *"working out"* the salvation that God has freely given to us. We must change who we are by allowing the Word of God to change what we think.

TESTIMONIALS

Unforgiveness-Bitterness

"My husband and I have encountered much spiritual opposition before we said, *"I do."* A lot of the attacks came from my family members and close friends on both parts. Not long after marriage, he and I began to slowly drift away from one another. I began to shut down emotionally and regret the day that I met him. There were many days I wanted God to rid me of this marriage. Days, weeks, months, and years passed by. I couldn't shake all the offenses that came from my husband and all those whom he associated with. I first was disappointed, then angry, and the anger turned into bitterness. It was so bad I couldn't recognize myself. I was losing myself in this ugly spirit of unforgiveness. I had allowed this hurt and pain to consume all my energy, time, and thoughts. I would complain to anyone who would hear just to release myself of the rage I felt. The cycle kept repeating itself and I did not know how to stop it. I did not know that this was a spot of unforgiveness.

When I identified it through *The Spot Class*, I was able to pray and ask God to help me. Through months of fasting, praying, worshipping, and surrendering to the Holy Spirit and allowing Him to deliver me from this spirit and heal the wounds, I can now say that I am free. I have forgiven my husband and released all those who have hurt me. I now make forgiveness a lifestyle. Glory to God!"

—*Monica C.*

Unforgiveness-Anger

"Going through this class made me realize that I was harboring a deep-seated anger towards my husband and son. I was angry toward my husband because I felt as though he did not see me or understand that I have felt rejected and neglected over all the years. Deep inside I know he loves me, I realize that he has never really learned how to show it. So, I have asked God for forgiveness and have begun to learn how to love unconditionally.

I was angry at my son because he is not perfect and because of his hearing and learning disabilities, I felt the neediness of it all. Again, I have asked God's forgiveness and to help me through the process to be more understanding and patient in my son's progress, so that he may grow more.

Once the realization of these feelings happened, it made me look at myself and the areas in which I need to focus on for my spiritual growth. By facing this *"spot"* and the damage it was doing to my total wellbeing, I know that when this rise of anger comes up to hold it captive, rebuke it, and know that the peace of God is in my soul."

—*Charlena B.*

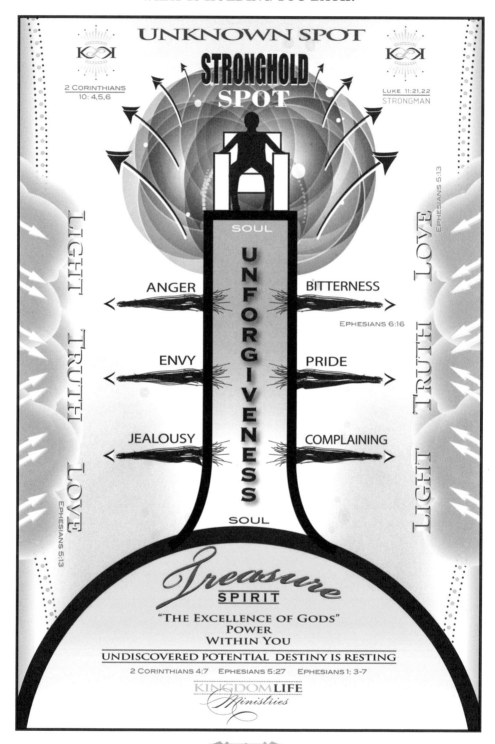

The Weapons of Our Warfare
To Confess and Bring Satan's Thoughts Captive

Unknown Spot
UNFORGIVENESS

ANGER

I John 3:15 (NKJV) Anyone who hates a brother or sister is a murderer, and you know that no murderer has eternal life residing in him.

Proverbs 15:1 (NKJV) A gentle answer turns away wrath, but a harsh word stirs up anger.

Colossians 3:15 (NKJV) Let the peace of Christ rule in your hearts, since as members of one body you were called to peace. And be thankful.

ENVY

James 3:16 (NKJV) For where you have envy and selfish ambition, there you find disorder and every evil practice.

Proverbs 14:30 (NKJV) A heart at peace gives life to the body, but envy rots the bones.

I Corinthians 13:4 (NKJV) Love is patient, love is kind. It does not envy, it does not boast, it is not proud.

JEALOUSY

Galatians 5:19-20 (NKJV) The acts of the flesh are obvious: sexual immorality, impurity and debauchery; idolatry and witchcraft; hatred, discord, jealousy, fits of rage, selfish ambition, dissensions, factions.

Galatians 5:22 (NKJV) But the fruit of the Spirit is love, joy, peace, forbearance, kindness, goodness, faithfulness.

Unknown Spot
UNFORGIVENESS

BITTERNESS

Hebrews 12:15 (NKJV) See to it that no one falls short of the grace of God and that no bitter root grows up to cause trouble and defile many.

Ephesians 4:32 (NKJV) Be kind and compassionate to one another, forgiving each other, just as in Christ God forgave you.

PRIDE

Proverbs 16:18 (NKJV) Pride goes before destruction, a haughty spirit before a fall.

I Peter 5:5 (NKJV) In the same way, you who are younger, submit yourselves to your elders. All of you, clothe yourselves with humility toward one another, because, "God opposes the proud but shows favor to the humble."

COMPLAINING

Philipians 2:14 (NKJV) Do everything without grumbling or arguing.

I Timothy 6:6 (NKJV) [And it is, indeed, a source of immense profit, for] godliness accompanied with contentment (that contentment which is a sense of inward sufficiency) is great and abundant gain.

Satan's defenses start with a thought. Bring the thought captive and bring it into judgment by these scriptures and confess them and victory will surely come.

The Hidden Spot
Shame

W hile unforgiveness is the *"unknown"* spot, shame is the *"hidden"* spot. Most people who struggle with unforgiveness are unaware that they are harboring unforgiveness in their souls. From their perspective, they believe they have put the past behind them. They believe they have pushed through the pains of long ago. They believe they have risen above the betrayals of others and have healed from the wounds they once bore. They believe they have made things right between themselves and those who have offended them.

However, a person with the *"spot"* of unforgiveness is a person who is suffering from the lingering side effects of the unpleasant experiences of the past. He (or she) lives in a world dominated by anger, envy, jealousy, bitterness, pride, and a lifestyle of constant complaining. These unpleasant and unseemly habits don't just appear out of nowhere. They are the offspring of something that is more fundamental in that person's soul. They are the offspring of unforgiveness.

Unforgiveness, therefore, grows unchecked in our lives because it generally escapes detection. We don't know that we have a problem until symptoms start showing themselves by destroying our lives. Like the man who dies suddenly from a stroke because he has no idea that plaque has been collecting in his arteries, so the person with unforgiveness has no idea that unforgiveness is saturating his life until a crisis experience enables him to see his own fault.

Shame, on the other hand, does not operate this way. In fact, shame is exactly the opposite. People with unforgiveness usually don't know that they have a problem with unforgiveness while the people closest to them know that they do. People with shame almost always know that they have a problem, while others around them are often the last to know. Shame is that part of us that we intentionally hide from others for fear of disapproval or fear of being exposed.

Shame was the first consequence of sin in the Garden of Eden. After Adam and Eve ate fruit from the tree of the knowledge of good and evil, in violation of God's command, they hid from God, attempting to cover their nakedness with pathetic little fig leaves. When God pressed them to confess the rationale behind their fear and their vain attempt at clothing themselves, they finally admitted that they were feeling shame.

Sin is like mold: It thrives in certain environments. Mold requires warmth and moisture. It grows and spreads where the climate is warm and muggy. Sin, likewise, requires a certain kind of environment to grow and spread. It requires darkness. Sin takes root in those dark corners of our lives that we hide from the rest of the world. It grows in our hearts when we close off parts of ourselves to God and to those around us. Then, the more we hide from God and from others, the more we struggle with secret sins that others cannot see and deep inner problems that others do not suspect. If we aren't careful, these hidden sins and carefully concealed problems consume and destroy us without even knowing what happened or why.

Sin is like cancer in many ways. Often unseen until its final stages, cancer does its deadly work in the hidden places of the human body. It can often go undetected until it is too late to do anything because it has spread and contaminated other organs and even the blood and the bones themselves. If sin is hidden from the sight of others, it grows and spreads and takes on increasingly destructive expressions and contaminates our lives as well. Because sin is hidden, it breeds an inner sense of shame. Then, shame breeds a different kind of sin in our hearts. This is the endless cycle of sin and shame that dominates the lives of so many people; the *"spot"* that is carefully concealed even from those who know us best.

As mentioned previously, each of the primary *"spots"* will be driven either by the spirit of Balaam (greed) or the spirit of Korah (rebellion), but shame is influenced by both spirits. The strongman of shame preys upon our sinful inclinations toward greed because all the shameful things we do are to satisfy our selfish desires. He also preys upon our carnal inclinations toward rebellion because we do shameful things in willful violation of God's laws. In fact, the reason we feel shame is because we are living contrary to God's known laws and we are trying to hide what we know is impure and unholy. The strongman of shame keeps us doing in darkness what we would never do in light. The unholy sense of exhilaration that follows hidden sins can become addictive and imprisoning.

The stronghold of shame camouflages what we don't want people to know about our past or present. What gives birth to this stain in our souls? What causes us to fall into trying to hide our sins from God, even though we feel conviction in our hearts and we must face them in judgment? What motivates us to think we can hide these things from the people who know us? What causes us to believe that we can conceal our sins forever?

Once again, it is the un-renewed areas of our mind that are breeding ground for shame. It is our lack of transforming to God's thinking that create the conditions for shame to thrive in our lives. Spiritual things are never birthed in a vacuum. There is something within the sinful nature that gives rise to sin in our lives. When we are unaware of sin's secretive work in the invisible places of our souls, the problem grows, spreads, strengthens and intensifies. It eventually consumes and dominates us, never allowing us to achieve our full potential in life. Like heart disease or cancer, the sickness of shame is often well advanced and deeply entrenched by the time its symptoms become apparent. By then, only drastic intervention can save us. It is important to recognize the warning signs as early as possible.

The symptoms of shame in our lives are rebellion, a deep need of controlling others, cursing, deception, self-centeredness, masking, and love for money that leads to evil thoughts and deeds. These *"defenses"* manifest in ways that are both subtle and obvious in the lives of people who are riddled with shame.

Rebellion is the prideful uprising of a person's will to thwart the authority that God has placed over his or her life. People with shame secretly detest accountability. Yet, they publicly proclaim the need for moral standards and personal responsibility, and they openly praise the benefits of such things. In private, they hide from authority figures God has placed over their lives because the authority will uncover the hidden source of shame and challenge it.

Pride is also present in the life of the person with shame. No one—especially the person hiding something—wants to be brought into the light and rebuked or humiliated in public view. The person believes they can *"manage"* the problem. He or she believes that their situation is *"different"*, and God *"understands"* their special circumstances. An ungodly sense of self-sufficiency, self-centeredness, and conceit often rules his thinking, keeping the messengers of truth God sends from penetrating Satan's defenses or gaining access to the *"spot"* of shame that rules his life. This person is unable to attain freedom from Satan's grip on the soul due to the unrealistic and exalted opinion of self that he or she holds.

A person bound by shame has a controlling temperament that is unnatural and excessive. He (or she) feels a compulsion to control others or restrain others in their individual pursuits in life. Control is the by-product of fear. This is because a person with hidden shame fears the consequences of being found out. For this reason, the person with a defense of shame will subconsciously turn the tables and try to control others since he cannot control himself.

People with shame also tend to curse a lot. They use inappropriate language to mask troubles in hidden areas and to vent frustrations because of being held captive by their secrets. So, deception follows this person. While he uses foul language and excessive exaggeration to make his points in dramatic fashion, he also misleads people and traps them into believing things about him that are not true.

A person with deep-seated shame tends to be selfish. A lifetime of nurturing a shameful *"addiction"* or a disgraceful secret has taught this person to focus on himself and elevate himself above others, even above the Lord. The obsessive pursuit of money often becomes an outlet for him, an activity that enables him to temporarily release all his pent-up frustrations and temporarily ease the inner sense of failure that haunts him.

All these problems and prevailing attitudes are merely deflections, distractions from the real issue that Satan does not want this person to uncover in his own life. The real thing Satan wants to protect in this person's soul is the hidden *"spot"* that destroys his appetite for excellence, thwarts the will of God for his life, and keeps him incarcerated in a dark and lonely prison cell of hopelessness and perpetual failure. Shame is a painful emotion caused by a strong sense of guilt, embarrassment, and unworthiness. When Satan can succeed in taking away a person's self-worth, he succeeds in taking away that person's destiny and earthly potential. If you are not in touch with the *"defenses"* that Satan employs to fan the flames of shame in your soul, you will be with the symptoms.

Deborah grew up in a large family with six children. Her father was a wealthy man, the owner of the most successful chain of funeral homes in one of the largest cities in Pennsylvania. On the surface, everything in Deborah's life appeared to be perfect. However, things were not what they seemed to be.

Deborah's home was a cold place emotionally. Her father was a stern and inflexible man who would severely beat her and her brothers and sisters at the drop of a hat. Running his household like a military base, Deborah's father expected perfection from every member of the family. If the children didn't produce straight A's on their report cards or if they failed to follow through with other things their father demanded from them, they were severely punished.

What Deborah didn't know until she reached her teenage years is that her father and mother weren't actually married. In fact, Deborah's father was married to another woman. He was married to Deborah's mother at one time, but her parents divorced, and her father married another woman. Nevertheless, he continued to come to Deborah's home at least once each day. Her father spent so much time there, never leaving until the children went to bed. Deborah and her siblings didn't realize that their parents weren't married until they became old enough to figure things out for themselves.

Deborah's father was consumed with appearances. He had to be. To maintain his respectable profile in the community and the business world, he had to maintain a certain image of respectability and protocol. He intentionally publicized the marriage to his new wife, but kept his children and former wife a secret from all those who knew him.

It never occurred to Deborah's father or the rest of those involved in this elaborate scheme, that the tangled web of deception was bound to unravel one day. Through her entire childhood, Deborah and her other siblings were not allowed to have friends. They were not allowed to go to school events, ballgames, or any type of social gathering that might give them an opportunity to talk about their home life.

Deborah was so distraught about her home environment and her father's physical and emotional abuse, she tried to commit suicide. In fact, she tried on two separate occasions to kill herself. If not for God's direct intervention, she would have died when she put a loaded gun to her temple and pulled the trigger, however the gun did not fire. Deborah was also beaten by her father when she pointed that same gun at him, due to the mental torture he was inflicting on her and her siblings.

Eventually, Deborah went to college, met a man, and got married. Her husband was in the military, and was transferred to a military base. Deborah moved with him to a much smaller city in the deep South and she experienced real culture shock for the first time in her life.

Being baptized and confirmed in the Episcopal Church in the northern United States, Deborah wasn't accustomed to seeing a church on every corner. She wasn't accustomed to the style of worship that was common in southern churches. Deborah's husband was a Nazarene, so she understood how difficult it was to blend two competing concepts of faith. Nothing could have prepared Deborah for the differences she experienced between formal liturgy (a big part of her childhood), and the passionate preaching and fervent worship that characterized small southern churches.

Deborah was also pregnant at the time. These monumental changes were overwhelming to her and greatly affected Deborah's life. Deborah and her husband started drifting apart and they eventually divorced.

By this time, Deborah had become a successful professional. If there was any benefit she derived from her father's stern approach and husband's military lifestyle, it was her heightened sense of self-discipline and determination. Deborah was extremely self-disciplined all her life. In fact, throughout elementary school, high school, and college, she was forced to be self-sufficient. In high school, she was an accomplished athlete, setting a national record in her event in track and field. Living alone with a child in a strange new culture was something that Deborah felt equipped to handle. All the while, Deborah continued to work hard to keep up appearances and keep the people in her life at a safe distance, so they would never discover the things that she wanted to keep hidden about her past.

A few years after her divorce, Deborah met a man and fell deeply in love for the first time in her life. Having convinced herself that this man was her perfect match, she began to spend all her money to make his life as wonderful as possible. She bought a $1 million home for the two of them to share after they became engaged, and she bought him expensive cars and other fine luxuries. Six years later, this man had not followed through with his promise to marry Deborah and eventually, she found out that he was cheating on her. The two of them continued to live together for a while, until he finally left her. Then, Deborah was alone again with her daughter.

That is when I met Deborah for the first time. Our professions caused us to cross paths, and I found her to be a highly competent, extremely intelligent, and motivated woman. So, while negotiating one of our business transactions, she began to question me about why I openly publicized the fact that my business was dedicated to

God. Deborah's exposure to faith had been limited to her experiences with an impotent and openly hypocritical church in a large city and southern entrepreneurs who proudly displayed Christian logos on their stationery and business cards yet showed no evidence of a life-changing encounter with Christ.

Just two weeks after her breakup with her fiancé, at a time Deborah now describes as the lowest point in her life, she asked me why I would openly advertise the fact that God is the actual owner of my business. She told me that she had found such claims by others to be laughable and self-serving.

That's when I told her, *"Jesus is misrepresented."* That simple statement seemed to make a real impact on Deborah, creating a situation where I could share Christ with her and talk about the true meaning of salvation. Eventually, Deborah surrendered her life to the Lord and started attending our church.

Shortly after coming to Christ, Deborah started to understand what God wanted to do in her life to make her whole. Deborah's bad experiences were awful and were plentiful. Satan had a grip on Deborah's life through the shame that had taken root in her soul. Deborah was so accustomed to living the whitewashed life to keep the truth about herself hidden, she really didn't know any other way to live.

When Deborah was a child, her father demanded that she help maintain the appearances he fabricated to sustain his reputation in the community. When Deborah got married, she was also expected to maintain her husband's reputation for the sake of his military career. When Deborah decided to pursue her own professional career in the wake of her divorce, it was important to her that everybody think highly of her and that they view her as a woman who was *"together"* in every sense of the word.

To hide her shame and conceal her problems and the unhappiness that surrounded them, Deborah learned to *"mask"* the truth about herself. As a child, she did this by avoiding the other children at school. She was not allowed to spend time alone with any of her schoolmates or invite any of them to her home. She was not allowed to attend any school functions outside the classroom, so the other children could never discover the true nature of her dysfunctional life. As an adult, Deborah took this same mindset of shame and habits of deception with her into college, her marriage, her subsequent engagement, and the isolation that followed because that was the way Deborah was used to living. These unhealthy practices and thought processes were keeping Deborah, even after her spiritual rebirth, from finding her rightful place in the world and fulfilling her true destiny in life.

Every *"defense"* that Satan is prone to utilize to protect his *"goods"* of shame were manifesting themselves in Deborah's life. Deborah was proud in an unhealthy and ungodly way. Over the course of the years, she learned how to masterfully conceal her problems, so people would think highly of her. She also learned how to create the appearance that her life was problem-free. Her grades were perfect in school and her athletic performances were perfect in her younger years. Deborah, because of the *"spot"* of shame controlling her life, did not want others to know about the personal and private undercurrents of hypocrisy that were governing her every decision and every move.

Deborah was controlling. She wanted more than anything to oversee her own destiny and dictate what other people thought about her. In fact, her *"image"* meant more to her than the truth. Deborah was instinctively deceptive. She was rebellious, too. She threatened her father with a loaded gun and lived with a man to whom she was not married, even though she knew that it is was immoral to do so, especially in the presence of her daughter.

However, God showed Deborah, not only His grace through salvation, but His power to deliver, as well. He opened her heart and mind to the truths of the Scriptures, so that Deborah could come to understand that, *"we have this treasure in earthen vessels, that the excellence of the power may be of God, and not of us."* *(II Corinthians 4:7, KJV)* That divine power within us by the New Birth is enough to change us and to set us free from our bonds.

This *"treasure"* that Paul writes about, that Deborah experienced in her personal struggle with shame, is the power of the Spirit that resides within us due to God's work of grace in our hearts. The *"treasure"* is the excellence of God's power and it is a power that excels or surpasses all-natural ability. It is the resurrection power that comes forth when we die to the strongman and his defenses and become alive to God through faith. Because this power is divine, not human in nature, it equips us with the ability to tear down spiritual strongholds in our lives that we could never have recognized before we were saved.

Our covenant promise as children of God is to walk in the blessing of Abraham. According to Paul, the blessing of Abraham is God's Holy Spirit in our lives *(see Galatians 3:14)*. So, to live and walk in the Abrahamic promise is to live and walk in resurrection power. The same Spirit who raised Jesus from the dead is alive in all true believers today *(see Romans 8:11)*, equipping them with both the desire and the ability to hear the Word of God in a new and life-changing way, understand it, and apply it to their own personal struggles. As people systematically tear down the strongholds that Satan has erected in their souls and send the strongman into exile, he can no longer manipulate them through their points of weakness.

Peter explained this same principle in another way when he wrote, *"His divine power has given us everything we need for a godly life through our knowledge of him who called us by his own glory and goodness. Through these he has given us his very great and precious promises, so that through them you may participate in the divine nature, having escaped the corruption in the world caused by evil desires." (II Peter 1:3-4, NKJV)*

It is the *"divine power"* within us that gives us all things that pertain to a godly life. It is the *"divine power"* within us that enables us to recognize the *"spot"* of shame in our souls and overcome its influence, as we abolish its dominance over our lives.

This *"divine power"* comes *"through our knowledge of him."* In other words, that kind of power does not naturally reside within us. We must come to know God in a personal, experiential, and life-changing way and we must become temples of his Holy Spirit before we can ever hope to defeat something as strong and imperceptible as shame. When we come to a personal knowledge of God, we have all the power we need to overcome all destructive experiences of the past and change all destructive thinking of the present.

Therefore, knowledge is the key. We see this over and over in the Bible. We must know God before we can walk in His promises and power. We must gain knowledge that only the Bible can impart and only the Holy Spirit can reveal to us before we can *"participate in the divine nature."* When we know the Lord and when we gain knowledge through His Word, we finally connect ourselves to those *"great and precious promises"* that He has made available to us.

Does this mean that a little *"spot"* of shame can keep us from the abundant life that God has promised to us? Does this mean that the hidden struggle we have with shame can abort the destiny to which God has called us? Absolutely! That is why Paul wanted us to have the knowledge we need about Satan's devices. The Lord has given us the necessary spiritual power to overcome the enemy's tactics. The Bible warns us repeatedly about the consequences of living under Satan's control. God has set before us a glimpse of what our lives can be like without the crippling effects of shame.

Writing to Christians in the first century, John said, *"If we claim to have fellowship with him and yet walk in the darkness, we lie and do not live out the truth. But if we walk in the light, as he is in the light, we have fellowship with one another, and the blood of Jesus, his Son, purifies us from all sin." (I John 1:6-7, NIV)* The things that happen in secret places are equated with lies in the Bible. Those who lie, whether intentionally or by hiding the truth from themselves and others, are walking in the darkness. Believers know the truth because the truth is within them, but they are not *"living out"* the truth, so they are not living under God's blessing and favor. Believers will never live under God's blessing and favor until they allow the Word of God to shine light upon the truth. Only then can they respond to it by tearing down Satan's stronghold, exposing all the inner sickness that shame has inflicted upon them. Then, God can heal that inner sickness and build strength where weakness once ruled.

How do you know whether you are currently *"in the dark"* or *"in the light"* when it comes to the deep, personal things of your life? You know by the company that you keep and by the relationships you pursue. The human soul naturally seeks the companionship of other like-minded people. If there are hidden things of darkness in your life, such as shame, you will naturally migrate toward other like-minded people and naturally avoid those who can see through your defense mechanisms. If the light has shined upon the dark places of your soul and you are making your way toward wholeness, you will seek an open relationship with God and with other Christians who have fought the good fight ahead of you. The good news is that even if you are currently walking in darkness to hide your inner struggle with shame, you can end this seemingly endless battle, as Deborah did by replacing your shame with true intimacy with God and others. You can turn this ship around.

In, I John 2:8, the verse immediately following John's observation about darkness and light, John explains that *"the darkness is passing, and the true light is already shining." (NIV)* So, the light of God is already shining in us, His children. It is shining in our spirits. The Word of God must make a *"connection"* with that light, so our minds can become enlightened, as well. In the end, the battle is won or lost through our thinking. It is vital that we understand what is happening within us as we struggle with the shame we hide from others and the truth about those things that give rise to our shame.

We know that shame is a hidden stain that infects every human soul because shame was the first and most enduring consequence of Adam and Eve's sin in the Garden of Eden. We are told in Genesis that immediately after they had eaten the fruit from the tree of the knowledge of good and evil, Adam and Eve took fig leaves and sewed them together in a vain attempt to conceal their moral failure. God went searching for the man and woman. He found them the same way that He finds us all. When God questioned them regarding their strange efforts to hide from Him, Adam told the Lord, *"I heard you in the garden, and I was afraid because I was naked; so, I hid." (Genesis 3:10, NIV)*

God knew the truth. He knew that human beings don't hide from Him or from each other unless they have something to conceal. People don't hide unless shame eats at their souls. Adam and Eve's sin caused them to lose God's covering over their lives and they tried to cover themselves in a vain attempt to obscure the disgraceful thing they had done. What vanity! God knew the truth all along, and so did Adam and Eve. Even the serpent knew what they had done.

Shame is a contamination that causes us to do senseless things. It is a blemish that causes us to believe we are invisible to God and to others when they can see right through us. Shame can be caused by several factors. Yes, it is the direct result of our willful sins and our acts of rebellion, but it can also stem from something that is not our fault. Often, shame is the consequence of something that was done to us or against us, something we could not control, yet it took away a part of our innocence.

We can't control the lifestyle of our parents. We can't control rape or physical abuse against our bodies, especially when we are young and vulnerable. We can't control the personal betrayal or willful acts of adultery committed by a disloyal husband or unfaithful wife. We can't control the lust, hatred, resentment or animosity that people may harbor in their hearts against us. We can't control these things. Nevertheless, the knowledge of these things can infect us with debilitating shame.

Shame is a painful, crippling emotion caused by an overpowering sense of guilt, embarrassment, remorse, or unworthiness. Shame may be warranted by hideous acts that bring deplorable consequences. Most of the time, the shame that inflicts real torment upon the soul and real damage upon our lives is shame that is unwarranted. It is associated with acts committed against us, not by us. It is associated with deeds we performed or words we spoke in the distant past, not of our present lives. It is associated with things we have done that we would never do again because our hearts and minds have changed toward those things *(this is the definition of repentance)*. The power of shame is found in its ability to linger long after the acts that gave rise to it have evaporated into the heavy fog of time.

The *"spot"* of shame is the residue of the fall of Adam and Eve in our lives. It is our innate response to the feeling of guilt that we naturally bear in our hearts before God. Remember, if you are saved, your spirit is free from sin and from the judgment associated with sin. Shame should not affect you because you have been reconciled to God through grace.

Nevertheless, the soul of man is still strongly influenced by guilt, so the soul is still strongly influenced by shame. The lingering presence of shame in your soul is the *"spot"* upon which Satan focuses as he tries to reestablish his foothold in your life. Remember, Satan's primary goal is to impede your spiritual growth and frustrate the forward thrust of God's kingdom through your life. That is why Paul said, ***"Work out your salvation with fear and trembling." (Philippians 2:12, NKJV)*** The power that you need to overcome shame and grow beyond it is a power that is already within you. You must allow the liberating light of God's Word to shine in the dark, shameful places of your soul so the power of God that is resident within you can *"spill over"* and impact your thinking, setting you free from the lingering effects of shame.

Remember, a *"spot"* has no power in or of itself, but we give it power by surrendering to it. We give it power by clinging to it and by yielding to the defenses that Satan employs to protect it. We give power to shame by living an undisciplined life of rebellion, pride, and deception. We give it power when we attempt to control how we look to people or what people think about us. We give it power when we *"mask"* over the truth so people will think more highly of us than they ought (***see Romans 12:3).*** If you are prone to these and other manifestations of shame, learn to recognize the tactics Satan uses against you and learn to submit your thoughts and behaviors to the Lord, until He breaks the power of this stronghold in your life and liberates you to walk in joy and to run in strength.

Obviously, the devil is not going to allow you to break free from his tightfisted grip without putting up a fight because he has invested a lot of time and effort in you. When you attempt to make changes, he is going to attack you in this area when you are weak, vulnerable, and most susceptible to his devices. He will place you in situations where the tension and stress will merge to stir up old feelings of pride and the ensuing need to *"mask"* the realities of your life. He is going to thrust you into situations where temptation abounds, so you will return to your old ways of thinking. Whenever a believer submits a new part of his life to Christ, Satan is going to do everything possible to strengthen his position in that person's soul, to thwart the person's efforts to grow.

When promotion is in motion, the devil is at work. When promotion is in motion, the enemy is always nigh, but the choice is yours. You have the power and must always remember that fact. If you align yourself with God's Word, you will eventually and inevitably succeed. If you align yourself with Satan and the residue of sin that is so familiar to you, you will continue to be dominated by shame.

God placed within you a desire for his promises. Embedded within your created nature is an innate hunger to see all of God's promises fulfilled in your life. The hidden *"spot"* of shame, like the unknown *"spot"* of unforgiveness, is Satan's "right" to hold you back from God's promises. It is Satan's *"claim"* to keep you under his thumb. Shame finds its power in the eight *"defenses"* that Satan employs to keep you trapped on the merry-go-round of disgrace, dishonor, and indignity.

My advice to you is the same advice that Deborah employed to break the death grip of shame upon her life: Identify those specific manifestations of shame that govern your thinking—one at the time—then, learn how to stop yielding to those manifestations. Learn how to stop yielding to your tendencies to *"mask"* who you are. Learn how to stop yielding to your inclinations to deceive people for the sake of appearances. Learn how to submit to godly authority instead of rebelling against everything that puts limitations on your behaviors. Learn how to stop controlling the people around you and how to view life through the eyes of others instead of from your own limited perspective.

What you feed, grows; and what you starve, dies. Begin starving the strongman of shame, and his grip upon your soul will start to weaken. Start nourishing your soul with the truth of God's Word, and the Lord's influence upon your thinking will increase. It's that simple, yet it's that profound.

To overcome shame and every other ailment that plagues your soul, keep your eyes on Jesus, *"the champion who initiates and perfects our faith. Because of the joy awaiting him, he endured the cross, disregarding its shame. Now he is seated in the place of honor beside God's throne."* *(Hebrews 12:2, NLT)* The Son of God himself was not immune to shame, but He endured *(tolerated and pressed through)* the shame and the humiliation of the cross because He was able to see what was on the other side. He was able to see beyond the temporal pain associated with that wooden *"tree"* to the glory, majesty, and dominion that awaited Him on the forefront of his suffering.

Like Jesus, you can overcome the power of shame in your life if you bring yourself to see in your own mind's eye the joy that awaits you when shame's stronghold is finally broken. Like Jesus, you need a revelation of what awaits you on the other side of your shame before you can break free from the grip of shame upon your soul. You need a supernatural glimpse into the kind of life and destiny you can have when shame no longer governs you.

Shame for the unbeliever is understandable. It is the natural consequence of a life that is lived in opposition to God, but shame for the believer is an oxymoron. The man who is forgiven has no need to hide in shame. The man who is declared righteous has nothing to conceal from God or himself. The man who belongs to Christ no longer belongs to the darkness.

TESTIMONIALS

Shame-Pride

The defense I have most identified with is the defense of pride in shame. When the teaching of pride went forth, I felt the conviction of downing someone and lifting myself above them.

I knew immediately that it dealt with putting down my manager at work. I would find myself with my co-workers talking about how he doesn't do certain things and his manager skills were awful. I went home, took communion, and asked for forgiveness. The scripture that came to me was *1 John 4:20, NKJV "How can you say that you love God and hate your brother. Whoever claims to love God yet hates a brother or sister is a liar. For whoever does not love their brother and sister, whom they have seen, cannot love God, whom they have not seen."*

I realized that not only was he the manager, but he was also a born-again believer. This made me realize that my shame was that he had accomplished so much in a short period of time. It allowed me to see that I had shame of what I had not accomplished in my life at the age that I am. I began to go to work and serve the manager. When conversations came up to talk about how bad he was, I began to speak in honor about him. The coworkers then began to say, *"You always defend him"*. It is amazing how God can turn things around as if they never happened. I came to the point of accepting the truth that one is not better than another because of what they have accomplished in life. All people are the creation of God and must be seen as such.

—*Kenric S.*

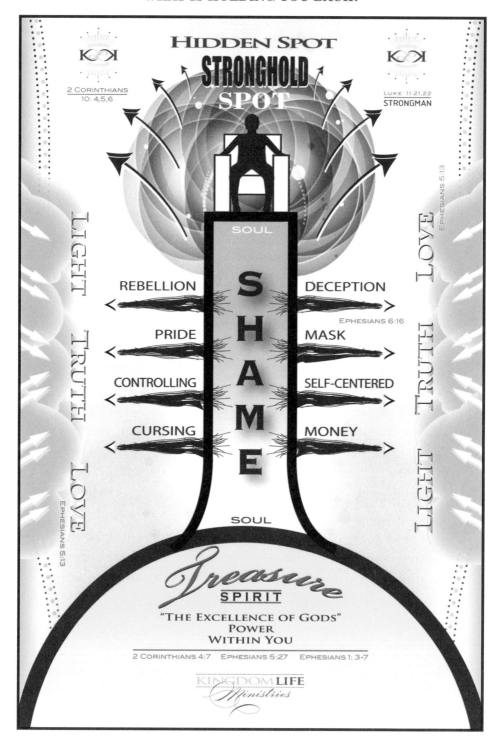

The Weapons of Our Warfare
To Confess and Bring Satan's Thoughts Captive

The Hidden Spot
SHAME

REBELLION

I Samuel 15:23 (NKJV) For rebellion is like the sin of divination, and arrogance like the evil of idolatry. Because you have rejected the word of the LORD, He has rejected you as king."

Psalm 68:6 (NKJV) God sets the lonely in families, he leads out the prisoners with singing; but the rebellious live in a sun-scorched land.

James 4:7 (NKJV) Submit yourselves, then, to God. Resist the devil, and he will flee from you.

PRIDE

Proverbs 16:18 (NKJV) Pride goes before destruction, a haughty spirit before a fall.

I Peter 5:5 (NKJV) In the same way, you who are younger, submit yourselves to your elders. All of you, clothe yourselves with humility toward one another, because, "God opposes the proud but shows favor to the humble."

CONTROLLING

Philippians 4:6 (NKJV) Do not be anxious about anything, but in every situation, by prayer and petition, with thanksgiving, present your requests to God.

I Thessalonians 5:11 (NKJV) Therefore encourage one another and build each other up, just as in fact you are doing.

The Hidden Spot
SHAME

CURSING

Exodus 20:7 (NKJV) You shall not misuse the name of the LORD your God, for the LORD will not hold anyone guiltless who misuses his name.

Colossians 3:8 (NKJV) But now you must also rid yourselves of all such things as these: anger, rage, malice, slander, and filthy language from your lips.

Proverbs 18:21 (NKJV) The tongue has the power of life and death, and those who love it will eat its fruit.

DECEPTION

II Corinthians 11:14 (NKJV) And no wonder, for Satan himself masquerades as an angel of light.

Psalm 101:7 (NKJV) No one who practices deceit will dwell in my house; no one who speaks falsely will stand in my presence.

John 14:6 (NKJV) Jesus answered, "I am the way and the truth and the life. No one comes to the Father except through me."

MASKING

Matthew 23:28 (NKJV) In the same way, on the outside you appear to people as righteous but on the inside you are full of hypocrisy and wickedness.

John 15:3 (NKJV) You are already clean because of the word I have spoken to you.

The Hidden Spot
SHAME
SELF-CENTERED

James 3:16 (NKJV) For where you have envy and selfish ambition, there you find disorder and every evil practice.

Matthew 16:25 (NKJV) For whoever wants to save their life will lose it, but whoever loses their life for me will find it.

MONEY

I Timothy 6:10 (NKJV) For the love of money is a root of all kinds of evil. Some people, eager for money, have wandered from the faith and pierced themselves with many griefs.

Deuteronomy 6:5 (NKJV) Love the Lord your God with all your heart and with all your soul and with all your strength.

Satan's defenses start with a thought. Bring the thought captive and bring it into judgment by these scriptures and confess them and victory will surely come.

The Blind Spot
Rejection

R ejection is the part of us we cannot see, but if we suffer
with rejection, other people can see our problem quite
clearly. Rejection is like a blind spot in a side-view mirror
because it keeps us from seeing ourselves, our environment, and
relationships the way they appear. It keeps us from understanding
why we do fruitless, even self-destructive things in our lives.

Rejection is the emotional dismissal of another person or the
spurning of a person's efforts or affections. As any person with
a sensitive heart well knows, any kind of rejection—rejection in
one's social life, career, and especially in romance—is a feeling
that can be devastating. The most destructive type of rejection
is that which we harbor inside because of our past experiences.
It steals our happiness and haunts us when we are alone. It eats
away at our self-esteem and motivates us to devalue ourselves to
avoid future episodes of rejection.

The cold, hard truth is that rejection is a part of life. There will
be occasions when even the most confident among us will have
a job application rejected, a date request denied, or a good idea
scorned by a leader or superior. It is healthy to mourn for a season
over disappointing experiences, learn from them, and move on

with life. When a person cannot find a way to bounce back from such setbacks and renew efforts to propel his life forward, a *"spot"* of rejection begins to grow in his soul, making him subconsciously susceptible to the fear of repeated rejection.

Rejection can be blatant in nature, taking on the form of bullying, teasing, or public ridicule. Rejection also can be subtler, though just as potent, when people ignore us, avoid us, or give us the *"silent treatment."* However, the experience of being rejected is subjective. One person may be slow to recognize the obvious rejection that others can see quite clearly, while another person may perceive rejection that is not actually there.

One thing is for sure: A person with a wounded soul is much more likely to internalize rejection, improperly process it, and allow it to consume his thinking. This affects the way he lives his life, particularly the way he relates to other people. Misdirected rejection leads to internal problems that flow from a warped sense of one's own value and worth.

Because of the social nature of human beings and complicated nature of life, the need for interaction with other people is instinctual and necessary. Simple interaction with other human beings is not enough to fulfill our deepest needs. Instead, we need to form and maintain deep emotional ties with other people. We tend to view our acceptance by others as a judgment of the worthiness of our lives.

Consequently, rejection is one of the most significant threats to a person's overall wellbeing because our happiness is closely linked to our social approval. According to the *Journal for Social and Clinical Psychology* (1990), most human anxiety seems to flow from concerns over social exclusion. Rejection—especially rejection experienced during childhood—can lead to patterns of aggressive or disruptive behavior, inattention, immature actions, depression, and extreme social anxiety that can haunt a person for the rest of his life because it is difficult to overcome. In fact, an analysis of fifteen school shootings between 1995 and 2001 revealed that peer rejection was a factor in 87 percent of those shootings.

Social psychologist Kip Williams, in his book, *Ostracism: The Power of Silence* proposes that rejection threatens four of our most basic human needs: the need to belong, the need for control in social situations, the need to maintain high levels of self-esteem, and the need to have a sense of a meaningful existence. Because these needs are so fundamental, and rejection poses such a threat to achievement, it creates a great deal of psychological distress and pain for the one who suffers from it. Consequently, according to Williams, people will do things they would not ordinarily do to reduce the likelihood of further rejection or to increase the likelihood of their inclusion in relationships they want to pursue.

Rejection can be destructive to an individual's spiritual health because rejection creates patterns of behavior in a person's life that are both unhealthy and habitual. Worst of all, these behaviors usually operate on a subconscious level, so the person perpetrating them is typically unaware that he is being controlled by his own internal motivations for acceptance when he exhibits certain behaviors.

Our most severe encounters with rejection occur in childhood or in the intimacy of romance and marriage. Those who suffer from these harsh forms of rejection often bear the scars for a lifetime. Such people routinely suffer from frustration, intense anger, and jealousy. In addition, they can easily experience isolation, despair, and possible long-term depression. This explains why rejection is a favorite tool of Satan in his never-ending battle to thwart God's plan for our lives and to hinder us in our spiritual growth. The devil knows that a person carrying the baggage of rejection is a person whose hands are too occupied with his own internal problems to be fully engaged in God's purposes for his life. Because Satan was rejected from heaven due to his pride and rebellion against God, he now works to find acceptance in a person's soul by creating a *"spot"* of rejection there. As it is with the other *"spots"* that contaminate the souls of men, Satan protects his *"spot"* of rejection by encouraging certain behaviors. This will have the effect of dominating a person's life, strengthening the influence of rejection on that person's thinking and reaffirming Satan's claim on this aspect of the person's soul. Specifically, there are six manifestations of rejection that are self-destructive: man pleasing, materialism, mistrust, fear, manipulation, and sex for approval.

As I have explained, people who have been rejected in the past are inclined to do some strange things to avoid further rejection in the future. For instance, people with sensitivity to rejection are often reluctant to express their opinions. They tend to avoid arguments or any type of controversial discussions. They are reluctant to make requests or to impose upon others. According to research, they tend to overly rely on familiar people and situations, so they can carefully avoid encounters with strangers or lesser-known individuals who might reject them.

In other words, people with a *"spot"* of rejection in their souls will often go to great lengths to please or impress the people around them. They will try to please strangers to win their approval. They will even try to please the few significant people in their lives to keep those people close and avoid the risk of losing them. In fact, I would go so far as to say that the typical person suffering from rejection tends to place other people on the throne of their life, bowing to them and serving them as he would serve a tyrant who had the power of life and death over him. People suffering from rejection tend to turn other human beings into idols, and themselves into puppets to obtain favor, approval, and acceptance of the people whose companionship they crave so intensely.

People suffering from deep-seated rejection also tend to be materialistic. This makes a lot of sense if you think about it. What better way to gain the acceptance of your high school classmates than to show up at school wearing the latest fashion trends? What better way to gain the attention of the young ladies at college than to pull into the dormitory parking lot in a new Ferrari convertible? What better way to impress your coworkers and professional colleagues than to arrive at the annual Christmas party with your *"trophy"* wife or husband? What better way to stand out at your profession's national convention than to boast about your yacht or your condo on the beach or your house in the city's most desirable neighborhood?

People with the *"spot"* of rejection tend to do things designed to help them cope with the wounds of the past, while avoiding the risk of being rejected again in the future. They tend to buy, buy, buy to prove their worthiness and merit and make themselves happy, because deep inside they can never quite get over the young girl who rejected their invitation to the school dance in the seventh grade. They tend to buy, buy, buy to fill a void that started early in life and continues to nurture a spending habit that can easily become self-destructive. They are never satisfied with what they own or what they have achieved. They are desperate to prove their worth as human beings and their value as people to be respected and desired. Rejection breeds materialism and mistrust because rejection is born out of insecurity.

Psychologists have proven that rejection is rooted in childhood experiences. If those painful experiences are inflicted upon a child in a recurring manner by multiple peers and adults, rejection can easily start to shape the way that the child perceives himself and how he approaches the life that God gave him. Unfortunately, nothing will change the distorted mindset unless the rejected child grows up and has a revelation concerning the true nature of his problem and how his twisted thinking is adversely affecting his life.

In the meantime, however, that child will be constantly suspicious of others and will grow into an adult who is constantly suspicious of others, because deep inside, in the subconscious parts of his wounded soul, he will never be able to bring himself to believe that somebody could love him or be truly committed to him in romance, business, friendship, or any other way. Why? Because he is unworthy of love and acceptance! All his childhood experiences of rejection—by his parents, his classmates, and the other significant people in his life—have taught him that unless he performs to earn the approval of people, he will never be accepted because he is an undesirable person that others can do without.

This is a terrible way to go through life, but this kind of internal suffering is common in today's world. Many children lack self-esteem because too many parents don't know how to show proper love for their children and too many children bully and harass the weaker and more vulnerable among them. Our kids grow up learning to emotionally survive by sacrificing their own dignity to please those whose favor they seek and by buying things or achieving things for the sole purpose of gaining attention and respect. Consequently, far too many of our precious children grow up learning to mistrust the people around them, even the people who truly love them. Because their thinking is skewed, their spiritual growth is stunned, even if they are saved, and the destiny that God has written for their lives is vulnerable.

People with rejection live in a constant state of fear. Because they have been rejected in the past, they fear being rejected again. They become willing to do almost anything to win the favor of those with whom they desire to associate. They are genuinely afraid of people and they have difficulty being intimate because they don't trust people and they won't trust the deeper parts of themselves to anyone for fear of being snubbed. Insecurity rules their lives, and self-doubt governs all their decisions regarding their relationships. Then, worry and anxiety dominate their minds, keeping them in a heightened state of alert regarding the behaviors of those who can hurt them emotionally. Consequently, rejected people are usually depressed people, often clinically depressed.

Rejected people are master manipulators, too, because they must be manipulative to keep up the appearances they believe others will approve. Inwardly, they suffer from insecurity and anxiety, but they cannot allow the people around them to catch wind of this fact. Rejected people, though depressed on the inside, are quite devious. Much of what they do is part of an elaborate scheme designed to hide their flaws while accentuating the phony image of themselves that they believe they need to perpetuate to win acceptance. Keeping up this ploy can be quite costly for a person's self-esteem and quite unfulfilling since nobody truly knows the person who suffers from rejection and nobody truly loves him or accepts him for who he really is.

Finally, people with the *"spot"* of rejection also tend to be sexually promiscuous. They often are enslaved by a lifestyle of fornication, adultery, lust, or homosexuality, because sex to them is more than just a pathway to sensual pleasure. To a person with low self-esteem, sex is often something done to gain the approval of another person or something to vindicate past rejections by previous sexual partners. For instance, a boy who was rejected by the teenage girls attending his high school may grow into a man who is a womanizer because his sexual exploits give validity to the masculinity that those younger girls could not see and could not appreciate.

The man who never managed to obtain the love of his mother when he was a small boy or the approval of his father when he was a teenager, the woman who was abandoned by her parents when she was only a child, and the man who was forsaken by his unfaithful wife four years into their marriage are all candidates for Satan's counterfeit remedy for their pain. A counterfeit remedy that promises them love, approval, and acceptance if they will simply hide the truth from those around them and play a constant mental game of manipulation and deception to gain the approval that they need.

Sin is a terrible thing, and that is why God hates sin. God doesn't hate sin because it offends His dignity, nor does God hate sin because it breaks His heart. God is too big to be blindsided by the actions of mere mortals, and He is too powerful to be wounded by the moral failures of those who reject Him. In spite of what the world might think, God does not hate sin because He wants to keep us from having fun. God hates sin because it destroys our lives. Sin also can destroy the lives of those who are affected by our sin. God hates sin because of what it does to us and what it does to those who are impacted by it.

For instance, when a father wounds his son by rejecting him in some way, not only will the child be damaged by the pain his father inflicts upon him, but the father will be damaged, as well. Not only will the father's life be devastated by guilt, shame, and regret, but the son's life will be marred with the same feelings of remorse and guilt. Only the grace of God, therefore, will be able to redeem these two damaged souls from destruction, and only the grace of God will be able to turn this situation around.

The problems won't stop with the internal consequences of this father's sinful deeds. Like leaves in a windstorm, these sinful acts are destined to spread like an infectious disease as his wounded son grows into manhood, becoming a father who rejects his own son and who hurts other people because of his hidden fear, anxiety, low self-esteem, and need for approval. Sin is not *"fun."* Sin is an endless cycle, a perpetual merry-go-round of pain that we inflict upon ourselves and others, who, in turn, infect more people with the deadly venom that flows from their wounded souls.

Nobody knew rejection more intimately than Jesus. He was betrayed by Judas Iscariot. Peter denied even knowing Him, cursing at a young servant girl to add credibility to his open denial. Jesus' mother and His brothers and sisters sought for Him in the villages of Galilee because they were convinced He was insane. Then, the Father in Heaven turned away from Jesus while He was dying on the cross because the world's sins had been placed upon the Son of God.

The Lord understands the power of rejection and its inherent curse better than anyone. He understands how it feels to be betrayed by someone he trusted. He also understands, due to His confrontation with Satan in the wilderness, how tempting it can be to *"perform"* for others to gain their approval. Remember, Jesus could have easily avoided the suffering of the cross if He worked a timely miracle in the presence of those who had the power to release Him.

Unlike Jesus, we don't usually have the spiritual maturity and the foresight—especially when we are young—to deal with the trauma and the pain associated with rejection. Consequently, we don't respond well to the tests that this painful emotion can force upon us. Instead of confidently standing in the knowledge of who we are in Christ, we tend to develop strong internal emotions of non-acceptance and unworthiness. Instead of finding peace in our relationship with the Lord, we tend to withdraw from God and from those who truly care about us. We eventually become willing to violate our own boundaries, consciences, and our closely held values for the opportunity to gain the approval of those whose acceptance we seek. Over time, therefore, a *"spot"* of rejection can take root in our souls and grow as we cultivate our feelings of worthlessness and isolation.

For example, a young man who was rejected by his parents, then rejected by his teachers and his classmates in high school, a young man who was never accepted as part of the *"in"* crowd that he so admired during his adolescent years, may eventually find *"Miss Right"* shortly after graduating from college. Because of the *"spot"* of rejection that has grown to dominate his soul, his low self-esteem and his fear of further rejection could easily prompt this young man to approach a flourishing relationship with an attractive young lady in an impure and unhealthy way.

He starts by buying her gifts, too many gifts and gifts that are inappropriately expensive. He does this because he wants to please her, impress her and wants to awaken in her an interest in him as a possible boyfriend. He starts treating her *"special"* and starts going to extremes to honor her every request and to fulfill every fantasy of her heart. He doesn't do this out of love because there is no real love between them. At this early stage in their relationship, he acts solely out of fear and out of a deep inner need to be accepted by the kind of person who would have ignored him in the past. He acts because he is afraid of losing her or appearing unworthy of her attention. Therefore, he goes overboard in his efforts to look prosperous, generous, attractive, and successful.

Soon, the young lady responds by accepting his romantic advances, and the two of them start dating. It doesn't take long before the relationship becomes sexual. The sex is not motivated by love or even by lust as much as it is motivated by a need for this young man to gain the approval of the woman and to bond with her on a level that will keep her in a relationship with him that is destined to have little depth. With this goal in mind, our young man turns up the heat on his efforts to gain her approval by financially contributing to the promotion of her career and her lifestyle. He buys her a new car, and he moves her into a penthouse apartment in an upscale part of the city, where he hopes to soon move in with her.

Before the ink is dry on the lease, this young man starts dominating and controlling the young lady through fear, because he is suspicious of what she might be doing when he is not around. Deep in his heart, because of his anxiety and low self-esteem, he can't believe that this beautiful woman could truly love him or that she would be faithful to him when she has so many other invitations from so many other men, including men at her workplace. He starts following her, listening to her telephone conversations from the adjoining room, and reading her texts and emails to discover what she is doing with her time. He becomes devious and manipulative as he uses guilt and other dishonest tactics to guarantee that she remains attached to him and that she abandons her association with anyone who can threaten his special role in her life.

Rejection is a particularly gruesome travesty. Not only is rejection painful, but it breeds more rejection by causing us to act in ways that compel people to run away from us. They can't always put their fingers on the source of the problem, but people who are emotionally healthy in this area of their lives can quickly sense that something is wrong, and something is terribly disturbing about the man or woman who has been devastated by rejection. Rejection is behind a lot of reclusiveness, a lot of physical violence, and a lot of disturbing behavior in this world.

As Satan prompts us to display the expressions of rejection that are common among those suffering with this ailment, he is leading us down a path that is designed to strengthen his grip on our lives. He is leading us deeper and deeper into the bottomless abyss of darkness where dysfunctional behavior is common because rejection breeds unhealthy behaviors that breed further rejection, and the downward spiral can go extremely deep. If truth doesn't shed light on the ruinous patterns of behavior that stem from this dysfunctional way of thinking, every relationship we forge, especially those forged through manipulation and other expressions of insecurity, are doomed to fail. No relationship in life can produce genuine satisfaction for the person scarred by chronic rejection, because a person with this stain on his soul will do just about anything to be accepted and avoid further dismissals.

David was a strong-willed individual, self-made, tenacious, and extremely disciplined and motivated. In his early 30's, he already owned his own construction company. He was well on his way to creating a name for himself. At the relatively young age of 34, David met the Lord and had a dynamic, life-changing encounter that resembled Paul's conversion on the road to Damascus. One day, like Paul, David was hard at work, doing what he thought he was supposed to do with his life and trying to prove to himself and those around him that he was an exceptional person. The next day, he was radically sold out to Jesus and would never be able to return to his former way of life.

David's mother had often told David that she saw him as the most financially successful of all her children. David's mother also saw her son as the most unhappiest of all her children. David had always felt that, even though he was working hard to build his life the right way, he didn't really know where he was going. He loved a challenge and was trying hard to excel in every aspect of his life. Nonetheless, David's pursuit of perfection was failing to satisfy his deepest needs. Then he encountered Jesus, and the Lord started dealing with a problem in David's life. God started dealing with David's deep sense of rejection.

David grew up in the North, but the family eventually moved down South, where David's father took a job earning about one-third the income he had been earning up North. David's father was angry all the time. He was angry about his financial decline. He was angry with his own father, David's grandfather, who lived nearby. He was angry at life in general, believing he had been given a bad set of circumstances by the hand of fate. This underlying anger contributed heavily to the mounting friction and dysfunction in David's home.

David's mother did not work outside the house. She stayed home to take care of David and his brothers. In fact, David's mom didn't even have a driver's license, so she was totally confined to the small house where they lived. Consequently, she felt trapped, and she was always depressed and detached. There were no expressions of real love in David's house, and there was a lot of abuse. There was a lot of betrayal, too, because David's father cheated on his mother multiple times.

David, because he was the oldest child, became the focus of his father's rage. Whenever David's father began to feel anger stir in his heart toward his own father, his financial plight, or any of the many problems that confronted him on a regular basis, David's dad would typically direct his rage at his oldest child. David felt rejected from his mother because of her emotional distance from him and rejected by his father because of the physical and emotional brutality.

David developed a strong, independent spirit and became very driven to succeed. Rejection creates a deep, emotional demand to prove oneself worthy of another's love. At the tender age of 14, David was beginning to develop a strong desire for vindication but was also drowning his immediate sorrows in drugs and sex. He became addicted to narcotics while he was still too young to drive. At the age of 18, he got married and moved out of his father's house. David had his own children right away.

David's young wife was suffering from her own emotional problems because she was sexually abused as a child. With

David's emotional problems conflicting with his wife's emotional problems, the two of them were headed for disaster, and after twelve years of marriage, they divorced.

This turn of events devastated David, because rejected people tend to have few intimate relationships. When one of those close relationships ends—especially the most intimate relationship of all—that experience can be devastating for the person who needs constant approval and companionship.

David immersed himself in work, trying to distract himself from the rejection he felt from his failed marriage. He was still feeling that there had to be something more to life than just pain and heartache. After all, David knew nothing but pain because of his family life. Living at home with his father and mother was painful all the time, and now he was feeling the same kind of pain after the loss of his own marriage. In desperation, David turned to a palm reader. The palm reader told David that she would give him all the details regarding his future if he would pay her $12,000 in advance for her personal insights. To most people, this might seem like a huge amount of money for a worthless service, but David was desperate, and this woman could sense it. Besides, she had a demonic influence on her life that enabled her to accurately describe to David many details about his past that no person could have known without some sort of unearthly knowledge. David was already convinced of this woman's supernatural powers and that is when the woman asked him for the exact amount of money that David had remaining in his bank account following his divorce. Convinced that he was doing the right thing, David handed the last of his money over to this woman in exchange for her guidance and counsel. The psychic then began to reveal what David's future held and the further she went on, David saw that there was no *"good news"*. After two days of pondering on what the psychic said, he began contemplating suicide. He figured that life was nothing but a continuous series of disappointments and sorrows, so he decided to call it quits and just put an end to his misery and suffering.

That is when the sovereignty of God began to manifest in David's life. As he was about to take a knife to slit his wrist, David received a phone call from a friend of his, a former associate he had not seen in a while. This friend invited David to church. This man, having recently become a believer in Christ, began to tell David about the Lord and what God had done in his life. The man strongly urged David to come to church with him to see for himself what Jesus was all about.

David accepted the invitation and went to church with his friend, where David had his own life-changing encounter with Christ, an encounter that immediately turned his life around. As David was prone to do, he devoted himself to this amazing shift that happened to him. Overnight, he became a fiery and passionate worshipper, giver, witness, and student of the Word of God. He gave up everything to serve the Lord and everything to follow him. He surrendered himself without reservation to the lordship of Jesus Christ.

The residue of rejection remained in David's life because he was blind to this *"spot"* that always functioned behind the scenes and out of sight in the deep recesses of David's soul. He was blind to the influence that his past experiences were still having on him, and he could not see how the stain of rejection was affecting his thinking, behavior, and especially his interactions with other people. David would soon learn that salvation is not the point in the Christian journey where we achieve perfection; salvation is the point where God begins the lifelong process of perfecting us. David had a long way to go.

David was still looking for approval, something that rejected people tend to do without even thinking about it. That is when

David met a woman who seemed to be the ideal companion for him. She attended church, she was an Ivy League graduate, and she was a morally good person with a good reputation. David dated this woman for a while. In fact, he dated her for twelve years. Because of the blind *"spot"* that rejection created in his soul, it took him all those years to figure out that this woman, though religious and good-natured, was also very deceptive because she had been deeply affected by rejection herself.

The wedding that they were always talking about and planning was being continuously postponed, and it never actually took place. In fact, the last time David saw this woman was the day before their wedding when she once again asked if they could postpone the ceremony. That is when David woke up, realizing that it is possible to love some people too much. In fact, some people will reject you, even though you love them with all your heart. David certainly loved this woman too much, sacrificing his dignity and even his moral values to keep her in his life because he was possessed by a fear of losing her. Too many people had already rejected him, he didn't want to be rejected again.

David eventually discovered the presence of this *"spot"* in his soul. Through a powerful revelation from the Lord, he came to realize that he was blindly and subconsciously doing things that were detrimental to his own wellbeing and to his various relationships. He came to realize that, even as a believer, he was being driven by an ungodly inner compulsion that he never knew existed.

Because of his encounters with rejection, particularly as a child, David had been shaped by a hidden survival instinct that prompted him to pursue materialism as a means of filling the void in his life and impressing the people around him. Because of the fear of further rejection that haunted him from within, David found it nearly impossible to trust the people closest to him. Because of the subtle and unseen ways that rejection reshaped his thinking, his view of himself, and his earthly relationships, David was always seeking love, always depressed, and overly devoted to the people in his life, even to the point where he became willing to sacrifice his own needs and values to satisfy the needs of others and thus gain their approval for himself.

The one positive aspect of David's nature that became God's starting point for changing this sincere believer's life was David's insatiable appetite for the Lord. David wanted to know everything about God, so he continually feasted on God's Word. Eventually, God began to show David things about rejection and things about himself and his own distorted thinking that David knew he would have to address.

As David spent time with the Lord, the Lord opened his heart to receive new revelation and opened his mind to start thinking differently about his past experiences and how those experiences had affected him in unseen ways. David started to see the connection between the rejection he had experienced over his lifetime and the things he was doing subconsciously to protect himself from further rejection, David began to find his deliverance from Satan's grip.

David was sexually promiscuous. David was a man-pleaser in every sense of the term. David was materialistic. David was non-trusting, fearful, and manipulative since he was young. He had learned these things as survival tactics in a harsh world where rejection is common. He learned these things as defense mechanisms that could protect him temporarily from the pain of being snubbed by his friends or discarded by those he loved.

What David did not know until God opened his eyes to see it, was the fact that these learned behaviors were demonic in their origins. Satan's *"defenses,"* are the tactics that the devil had instilled in David's life to trap him. This thinking was designed to keep him oblivious to the truth concerning his problem; and it trapped him on a merry-go-round of repetitive behaviors fabricated to defeat him and demoralize him. He, in turn was blinded from seeing the bigger picture of his life versus the picture of his immediate emotional needs.

However, all that began to change when David realized that Jesus accepted him without conditions and that Jesus would never leave him or forsake him *(see Deuteronomy 31:6)*. The light of revelation began to shine in the dark corners of David's soul when he finally understood that Jesus loved him even when he was a sinner *(see Romans 5:8)*. David didn't have to do anything to earn or keep God's love. God's love was free and unconditional. It was permanent, too. This knowledge began to change the way David thought of himself and the way he viewed his other relationships. He started viewing his interactions with other people through the lens of his interaction with God, and that helped him to deal with his unhealthy tendencies and helped him to break the entrenched patterns of his unhealthy thinking.

Until the kingdom of love and acceptance replaces the kingdom of fear in your mind, you, too, will be trapped in a vicious cycle of distorted thinking and self-destructive behavior that gives rise to unhealthy relationships and to an unfulfilling life. Remember, if you are born again, everything you need to defeat the blind *"spot"* of rejection is already present within your spirit. The Word of God must activate what is in your spirit and impact your behavior through the renewing of your mind. Then the spirit, being saved, will produce a soul that is saved. Eternal life that awaits you in heaven can be partially realized today through an abundant life in this present world.

Know what the Bible teaches about rejection and the fear that generates it. Know what the Bible teaches about your own tremendous worth to God. Learn about Jesus, who was despised and rejected of men *(see Isaiah 53:3)* so he could identify with the rejection you faced as a child, as an adult in love, and as a person seeking proof from others of your own value and worth. When you do, the light that shines in your spirit will shine upon the dark places of rejection in your soul, leading you to your deliverance and to your complete emotional healing. The destiny that awaits you will no longer be hindered by an assessment of your own value and worth.

TESTIMONIALS

Rejection-Non-Trusting

I moved down South with my husband during our 7th year of marriage. This is my 2nd marriage as my first marriage ended in divorce. I was raised Catholic but was not a practicing Catholic, as did not agree with a lot of the things going on in the church. My spiritual awakening started after I moved to the south. I was introduced to the Bible as well as a whole new view regarding God, Jesus, the Holy Spirit and RELATIONSHIP.

Looking back, I think that I have always had the spot of Rejection. At the beginning of our marriage, my new husband would say (tongue in cheek), here we go again with your quarterly talk when I would start conversations with, *"If you ever cheat on me, the marriage is over. No second chance, as I would never be able to trust you again"*. I guess it is because I had insecurities from my first marriage as well as growing up in a divorced household when it was not the norm as it is today. Unfortunately, I was *"speaking"* out this fear. And, as we know, the power of the tongue is strong in the Kingdom, and every time we talk, we plant a seed in Life and Peace OR Sin and Death. I was planting a seed in Sin and Death.

In the 9th year, my father was very sick and because I had the flexibility of working from home, I moved with my father for two months to help him. While I was gone, I got a call from my neighbor on Halloween saying that my husband had a dinner party and she saw couples going into the house. She knew that I was away and wondered if I knew about the beautiful blond-haired girl who was with the group. I had no idea what she was talking about and told her that she must be mistaken. She kept saying *"why would I lie to you – what do I have to gain?"*. As she was talking to me, I could feel the insecurities rise and I was crushed. I called my husband, and started with, *"Do you have anything you want to tell me?"* My husband did not know what I was talking about, so when I described what the neighbor had said about a party, he still said, *"I truly have no idea what you are talking about"*. The calls went back and forth between me and my neighbor and me and my husband (who that day was in the middle of a few urgent deliverables from work). The neighbor kept harping on the *"beautiful blond"* and said, *"I even noticed that David had an extra skip to his step while coming home from lunch and quite a smile on his face"*, intimating that he and the blond-haired girl got *"along"* well.

At this point, I was devastated and started crying as I was getting confused. My husband kept saying, that *"it is a crazy story."* He doesn't even know the four couples to have over for dinner, and he was on the phone with me off and on during the night sending me text messages with pictures of his progress carving pumpkins. My husband finally put his foot down and said he was not wasting any more energy trying to defend himself because I should know him better than my neighbor.

Before all of this happened, I had been reading the Bible and seemed over the last few days, that everywhere I read in the Bible, the following words had jumped out at me: *"I AM your rock–your fortress, your firm foundation–your high-tower–your refuge–your shield..."* and also *"STAND STILL and know that*

I am God" and *"Don't look right or left–STAND STILL, and know that I am God"* All of a sudden in the midst of this chaos, I remembered those words and prayed *"God, I know that you would not have put my husband in my life as well as moved us down south without a godly purpose".* I kept saying over and over–*"JESUS, you are my ROCK, my FIRM FOUNDATION, my HIGHTOWER, my SHIELD…."* And I was immediately calm, and the crying stopped. I realized confusion is a strong sign that Satan is in this and that I am in the middle of a spiritual attack and a spiritual trial. Do I look UP and choose God and Jesus, or do I believe Satan and the lie? My entire demeanor changed, I truly had PEACE on the entire situation. I did not realize at the time, but God will always give you a revelation and a rhema Word BEFORE your trial, so that you stand on that Scripture DURING your trial.

In the end, I truly believe that people can have thoughts or visions put in their head, not only God-given thoughts and visions, but Satan as well. Satan is attracted to our dark spots whether we have given our lives to Christ or not. Even if we have given our life to Christ, we still have dark spots and residue left over from the unsaved man and our job is to partner with God, so we can be TRANSFORMED in mind, soul, spirit and finances. I am convinced, that Satan used my neighbor to put a vision in her head as he knew that trust and rejection issues were the crack in my armor. That was his way of entering to break up our marriage. The good news is that it gives me an indication of how important our marriage is to the Kingdom and that God *"KNOWS THE PLANS HE HAS FOR US, plans to prosper us and not harm us. Plans to give us hope and a future." (Jeremiah 29:11, NKJV)* I had to stand still and trust in the Lord. Satan wouldn't have wasted his time on breaking up our marriage if our marriage wasn't important to the Kingdom.

Understanding the spot of rejection and how it affects the mindset is helpful because you realize that *"our weapons of warfare are not carnal, but mighty in God for pulling down strongholds." (II Corinthians 10:4, NKJV)* I came to the realization that God would not have me in a marriage with a man that I could not trust. Even deeper, it wasn't about trusting my husband, but trusting God in the middle of my trial. He just wants us to CHOOSE HIM in the trial and not to pay attention to the worldly chaos swirling around during trials.

Going through *The Spots Class*, it was made clear exactly what happened. It was the spot of rejection and Satan was attracted to the rejection in me and would use it any way to tear apart what God had put together. But we must trust in the truth and not the lie, because the Bible says is, *"therefore, what God has joined together, let man not separate." (Mark 10:9, NKJV)*

I believe that I have matured in letting go of the thoughts, not that they don't come, but now I know how to take those thoughts CAPTIVE and measure them by the Word of God. I never would have known that this was a spiritual battle and I had to surrender it to God, learning to choose Him and not the lie.

—*Kimberly M.*

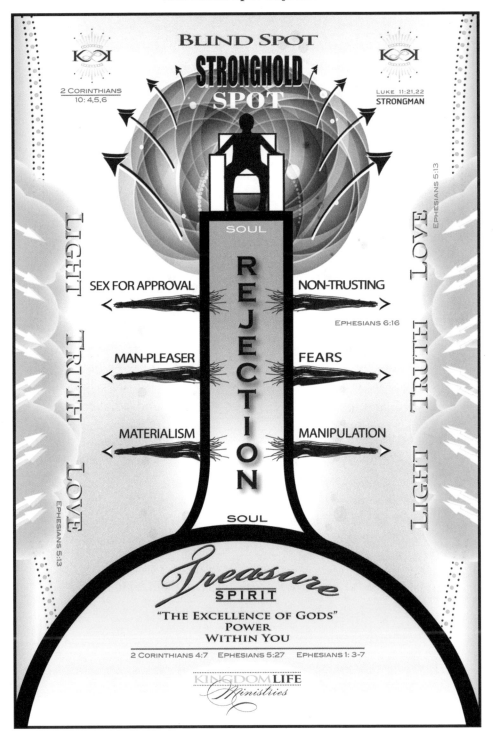

The Weapons of Our Warfare
To Confess and Bring Satan's Thoughts Captive

The Hidden Spot
REJECTION

SEX FOR APPROVAL

I Corinthians 6:18 (NKJV) Flee from sexual immorality. All other sins a person commits are outside the body, but whoever sins sexually, sins against their own body.

I Corinthians 6:13 (NKJV) You say, "Food for the stomach and the stomach for food, and God will destroy them both." The body, however, is not meant for sexual immorality but for the Lord, and the Lord for the body.

MAN PLEASER

Proverbs 29:25 (NKJV) Fear of man will prove to be a snare, but whoever trusts in the Lord is kept safe.

I Corinthians 7:23 (NKJV) You were bought at a price; do not become slaves of human beings.

MATERIALISM

Matthew 16:26 (NKJV) What good will it be for someone to gain the whole world, yet forfeit their soul? Or what can anyone give in exchange for their soul?.

I Timothy 6:6 (NKJV) Now godliness with contentment is great gain.

The Hidden Spot
REJECTION
NON-TRUSTING

Proverbs 28:26 (NKJV) Those who trust in themselves are fools, but those who walk in wisdom are kept safe.

Psalm 32:10 (NKJV) Many are the woes of the wicked, but the Lord's unfailing love surrounds the one who trusts in him.

FEAR

Job 3:25 (NKJV) What I feared has come upon me; what I dreaded has happened to me.

I John 4:18 (NKJV) There is no fear in love. But perfect love drives out fear, because fear has to do with punishment. The one who fears is not made perfect in love.

II Timothy 1:7 (NKJV) For the Spirit God gave us does not make us timid, but gives us power, love and a sound mind.

MANIPULATING

I Thessalonians 4:7 (NKJV) For God has not called us to impurity but to consecration [to dedicate ourselves to the most thorough purity].

Zechariah 8:16 (NKJV) These are the things that you shall do; speak every man the truth with his neighbor; render the truth and pronounce the judgment or verdict that makes for peace in [the courts at] your gates.

Advancing The Kingdom

In the three preceding chapters, you were introduced to three people I know personally. For purposes of this book, their names were changed to safeguard their privacy. Levi, Deborah, and David are living examples of the things God revealed to me in the three visions: Unforgiveness, Shame, and Rejection.

These visions and the correlating experiences of these three people serve to remind us of God's primary objective in our lives. Regardless of who we are, where we came from, or how long we have served the Lord, God's purpose is to advance His kingdom *in* our lives and *through* our lives. At salvation, we entered His kingdom. Entering God's kingdom is not the same as inheriting His kingdom, nor is it the same as enjoying the benefits attached to that inheritance. God's work in our lives after salvation is a work that is designed to bring us to spiritual maturity and perfection, and the Holy Spirit will continue this work for as long as we draw air into our lungs.

In fact, in Galatians, the apostle Paul teaches us that, because we are heirs of the kingdom of God, we are *"subject to guardians and trustees until the time set by (our) Father"* for us to receive that inheritance *(Galatians 4:2, NIV)*. The kingdom that we have entered through faith must be nurtured in us and developed in us. It must be expressed through us incrementally as we read God's Word, absorb it, and learn how to apply it to our lives. Therefore, through God's word we grow *"from glory to glory"* *(II Corinthians 3:18, KJV)*. The only device God consistently uses to teach us how to believe His Word and rightly apply it to our lives is a trial. Only by walking through the trials of life can God's people ever hope to learn God's ways, grasp God's wisdom, or incorporate God's mercy into their lives in a real, practical way.

That is why you and I experience trials. Levi, Deborah, and David experienced their own trials. My three friends navigated troubled waters in their lives, so God could put to death the *"old man"* *(Ephesians 4:22, KJV)* that dominated their thinking and their behavior to resurrect within them a new and godly way of perceiving life and experiencing it.

Before God can resurrect something in our souls, that *"old"* thing within us must die. That is what I want you to take from this book. I want you to learn by reading about the personal experiences of my three friends. The thing God wants to bury and pronounce *"dead"* in your life is the *"old man,"* so he can bring forth ***"the new man, which after God is created in righteousness and true holiness."*** *(Ephesians 4:24, KJV)* Once we are saved, we are destined to be sifted. God is allowing the *"spots"* in our soul to be illuminated, so that we can sift through to see what is of God and what is not. After we have been sifted, we are destined to be shifted. God is helping us, through His Word, to shift our patterns of thinking. Ultimately, we are lifted into the true purpose in which God has called us to. God's process for taking us to a higher spiritual plane is to first walk with us through the valley so faith and character can be nurtured in our souls and the *"spots"* and stains that contaminate us can be exposed, treated, and healed.

The apostle Peter wrote to the early believers, *"After you have suffered for a little while, the God of all grace, who called you to His eternal glory in Christ, will Himself perfect, confirm, strengthen and establish you." (I Peter 5:10, NASB)* This proves that sufferings and trials are temporary. It also proves that they are intentional. God allows trials in our lives for a purpose. It is up to you and me to decide whether we will embrace our trials to squeeze all the benefits out of them that God intended, or whether we will try to avoid the unpleasant trials of life by resisting them, fighting them, or cursing the day they came upon us.

No sane individual would ever be happy about being put in the crucible of testing, we should clearly understand that the trials God allows in our lives are there for a reason. As hard as it is to believe, trials are designed for our benefit. Although trials will not destroy the man who lives according to God's Word while he is enduring the temporary discomforts of his trial, they will help that man grow and achieve the destiny that God has planned for him, especially the spiritual destiny that can only be attained through the grace of suffering.

Trials are intended to move God's people from diapers to dominion and from the church age to the kingdom age, where the rule of God is manifested in our earthly lives as it is in Heaven. We know from the model prayer that Jesus taught us *(the Lord's Prayer)* that it is God's will for the Kingdom of Heaven to meet the Kingdom of God in our hearts. This meeting is accomplished in the soulish parts of man, where the *"old nature"* is put to death through the trials that God ordains for us, where the Word of God that has been sown into us finally produces its fruit in our thoughts, decisions, feelings, and affections.

The lessons we can learn from these three people I have introduced to you is that God allows trials in our lives. He allows specific trials that help us overcome specific problems, and His end goal is to put to death something destructive in our souls. Then, He can resurrect something heavenly and take us to a higher place in our relationship with him and our effectiveness in his work.

If you have *"spots"* on your soul that are holding you back in your journey toward spiritual perfection, God wants to eliminate them from your life. The device that He will use to achieve this goal is a trial, you will face because of the specific blemish that has left its mark upon your soul.

Because the soul has four parts—the intellect, the will, the emotions, and the affections—these are the parts of us that will be deeply affected by the *"spots"* that form because of our experiences. The human spirit is comprised of intuition, communion, and conscience. God's plan is to speak to your conscience and your sense of spiritual awareness through His Holy Spirit, but speak to your mind and heart through his engrafted Word. When the Word of God in your mind and the presence of the Holy Spirit in your inner being confront the stains and blemishes that contaminate your soul, a trial is inevitable. God's design, however, is to use your trials to eradicate the *"spots"* that contaminate your soul and resurrect the *"new man"* within you. God did this in Levi, Deborah, and David's lives. He desires to do this in your life, too. He desires to advance His kingdom in your life.

How do trials play out in our lives? How do they manifest themselves? How can we distinguish between a real trial designed for our benefit and an everyday problem we must confront as a simple byproduct of living in an unjust world? After all, we have all become accustomed to the conflict and the toil associated with everyday living, so we don't really think about the things that happen to us daily. We don't really think about the challenges we confront and how a simple problem can become an opportunity to either move forward or move backward in our spiritual lives.

The first sign of a real trial is the way in which that ordeal impacts our thinking. It is through our thinking that Satan launches his initial assault for the domination of our lives. Consequently, that is where the first volleys of hostile fire take place in any spiritual battle, because *"as (a man) thinketh in his heart, so is he." (Proverbs 23:7, KJV)*

In a powerful concept often attributed to Frank Outlaw, the founder of the *BI-LO* grocery chain. *"You should watch your thoughts because they become your words, you should watch your words because they become your actions, you should watch your actions because they become your habits, you should watch your habits because they become your character, and you should watch your character because it becomes your destiny."* So, thoughts are important. It is important what we think about God and what we think about ourselves. The other things we allow to dominate our thinking are also important because, in our minds, we create idols. In our thoughts, we create passions and lusts.

The question that each of us must ask is, *"Where is this thought taking me?"* In fact, I would go so far as to say that this question is more than just the *first* question we should ask ourselves; it is the *most important* question we should ask ourselves when we start thinking things that are contrary to God's way of thinking. If we can recognize a trial when it is in its initial stages and deal with that trial while it is still only a thought, we can save ourselves an enormous amount of suffering and an unnecessary abundance of pain.

When something goes wrong, or when somebody offends you, when a challenging situation comes along or when catastrophic news confronts you, the first thing you choose to do under those circumstances could be the most important thing you do in that trial. What you choose to think about in that situation and about the key players in that scenario *(including God and yourself)*, will go a long way toward telling you where your trial could take you. To think the right things is to overcome your trial more quickly and grow because of it. To think the wrong things is to repeat the same old patterns of suffering and spiritual stagnation that have dominated your life in the past. Every trial, therefore, is an opportunity to either move forward or move backward, to become bitter or become better. The choice is yours.

This goes back to one of the original premises of this book that I have been driving home to you repeatedly; namely, that the battle for your soul is waged in your mind. In your thinking, Satan either loses control of you or gains increased control over you. That is why it is so important that, as a Christian, you learn to follow the advice of Paul by taking captive *"every thought to make it obedient to Christ." (II Corinthians 10:5, NIV)* Nowhere is this more important than during an emerging trial because our trials become the turning points of our lives, the *"pivot points"* that either take us closer to God or farther from him.

Just think about it! The thoughts in your mind are like seeds in the soil. They WILL grow. There is no doubt about it. They WILL produce something. It is not difficult to figure out what those seeds will produce for you. In the physical world, a tomato seed produces tomatoes and a kernel of corn produces corn. It is precisely the same way with the *"seeds"* of your thoughts. Your thoughts will either produce *"death"* in some area of your life or produce *"life"* for you. They WILL produce one or the other. So, quit lying to yourself and quit pretending that your thoughts don't matter. Take your thoughts captive and submit them to Christ, particularly when it becomes apparent that your thoughts are taking you in a direction you don't really want to travel.

The Word of God, as I have explained, is your ally. In your battle against destructive thoughts, the Word of God is your weapon of choice. If you have saturated your mind with the wisdom contained in God's Word and stored that Word away in your heart, you will have the resources at the onset of your trial to recognize both the *"seeds"* of Satan's initial volleys and the potential outcome of aligning yourself with those thoughts through your words and your deeds. While the Word of God is your primary weapon in this battle, worship is your source of strength. Worshipping God strengthens us to cast down the damaging thoughts that invade our minds.

In, *II Corinthians 10:4-5 (NKJV)*, Paul told the believers in the Greek city of Corinth, *"For the weapons of our warfare are not carnal, but mighty through God to the pulling down of strong holds; casting down imaginations, and every high thing that exalteth itself against the knowledge of God and bringing into captivity every thought to the obedience of Christ."* From this statement, we can conclude that spiritual strongholds are established in our lives through our minds *(through our thinking)*. They are established through our *"imaginations."* Consequently, we must take every thought *"captive."* We must bring every thought under submission *"to the obedience of Christ."*

In other words, we must gain control over our own thinking and cause our thoughts to serve us rather than destroy us because thoughts are temporary even though they can do permanent damage. Thoughts are based on partial truths and flawed observations even though they can dictate the direction of our lives. Thoughts can wreak havoc in our relationships and expectations for the future because they are fueled by emotion instead of objective truth and they are driven by all that we *do not know* instead of what we *should know*. In the same way that Levi's thoughts fed and nurtured his unforgiveness, Deborah's thoughts of shame compounded to produce a deceptive lifestyle, and David's thinking about the many episodes of rejection in his life led to his desperate and destructive search for identity, your thoughts, if left unchallenged, have the power to take you toward a destination you really don't want to visit. Unless you can *"take captive"* these less wholesome thoughts that come into your mind because of the trials that beset you, you too will find that your thoughts give rise to additional *"spots"* in your life or to the fortification of the *"spots"* that are already present in your ailing soul.

The Word of God is your primary *"tool"* for tearing down strongholds of errant thinking and unfounded belief that impact every decision you make, every action you perform, every emotion you feel, and every affection you express. The Word of God is the most powerful mechanism for changing the way you think about yourself, about God, about life, and about others. The man who nourishes his soul daily on the Word of God is the man who will have the ability to recognize the stains that are present within his life and purge those stains from his being, so God can deliver him from their controlling power and heal him from their deceptive influence. The Word of God is your *"mechanism"* for attaining spiritual maturity and perfection.

While improper or unfounded thoughts are the first sign that a believer is entering a trial, the second sign of the presence of a trial are the words that come out of that person's mouth. After all, the thoughts in the mind are destined to express themselves through the words that we speak. Thoughts, though invisible, are real, so they eventually take shape and find their expression outside our minds, through our lips.

Words can be a bad thing, as we all know. Words can also be a good thing because they give us a clear view into the hidden recesses of the soul. In the same way physical symptoms can be an unappreciated blessing because they reveal hidden problems in the human body, so words can be a blessing because they can reveal hidden problems within the human soul. What's inside the soul is destined to come out of a person's mouth *(see Matthew 12:34; Luke 6:45).* Words that you speak as you enter a trial become the evidence of what is right and wrong in your thinking.

Your words also reveal those with whom you are *"fellowshipping"* and those with whom you agree. When you say, for instance, *"I am worried,"* you are revealing that you are fellowshipping with the enemy and you have come into agreement with his negative and hopeless assessment concerning your life. And when you say, *"I am anxious,"* you are demonstrating that you are fellowshipping with one who has filled your heart with fear because he has succeeded in filling your mind with doubt.

When you say, *"the Lord gives, and the Lord takes away. Blessed be the name of the Lord,"* you are showing that you have fellowship with the Father and you have come into agreement with His Word. You are showing that, even though you are resisting the temptation to live in denial as you confront your trial, you are convinced that God is in control of your life and He is holding you firmly in the palm of His hand. Nothing will happen to you that He does not allow.

According to the Bible, your breath is *"spirit."* When you speak something aloud, you give life to that thing you have spoken. If you speak the truth as it is revealed in God's Word, you give that confession power to affect the outcome of your trial and you endure that trial. If you speak from your soul those things that align you with Satan's lies, you give spiritual power to false ideas that have no real substance in and of themselves. They only have substance because you believe that they do, confess that they do, and act upon them as if they do.

Your words have the power to bring reality to a lie or to make the truth null and void in your life. In the same way that a person suffering from psychosis can harm himself because he is convinced that the imaginary voices he is hearing are real, so you and I have the power to harm ourselves by taking a thought that is objectively false and giving it the power of truth by embracing it and acting upon it. This happens when we confess false or impure sentiments aloud.

In fact, the word *confess* is an interesting little word. The root of the word, *"fess,"* comes from a Latin word that means *"to acknowledge, declare, or avow."* And the prefix, *"con,"* is a familiar prefix in the English language, meaning *"with."* To *"confess"* something is *"to acknowledge, declare, or avow with"* another person the same thing that he has already spoken. To confess God's Word, for instance, is to *"say with"* God the same thing that God has already said about a subject. To confess a lie or a deception of Satan is to *"say with"* Satan the lie that he wants to perpetuate.

Never is the temptation to do this greater than when we are amid a trial. During a trial, our words either support God or deny him; they either uphold the enemy or reject him. Our words either confirm in our hearts what God has already said about us and our circumstances or confirm what the enemy is saying to us right now. Through our words, we either align ourselves with Satan or we align ourselves with God. Through the sentiments that escape our lips, we reveal with whom we are fellowshipping and whose voice we are listening to.

I don't want to feed and nourish the devil. I don't want to help Satan promote something that is untrue or make one of his falsehoods effective in my life, it has no basis. I don't want to inadvertently help the enemy steal, kill, and destroy things in my life because I have empowered him through my unintentional endorsements. Instead of nourishing the devil, I want to starve him to death and deny him access to my life through my words. So, if I am fearful during a trial, I won't open my mouth to anyone but God. If I am worried, I won't tell anyone about my concerns. If I am angry, I will keep my anger to myself and give it no expression in my interaction with others.

Instead, I will make a deliberate effort to open my mouth and give expression to things that I know in my spirit are true, even though I may not be experiencing those things in my life at the time. I will praise God even when it hurts. I will worship the Lord even when I don't feel like it. I will give thanks in all things simply because God's Word tells me this is what I should do *(see 1 Thessalonians 5:18)*. I will give expression to the power of God in my life by *"saying with"* the Lord the same things He has already said about me, my situation, the key people who are part of my trial, and His own motives for allowing me to walk temporarily through *"the valley of the shadow of death." (Psalm 23:4, KJV)*

Have you ever wondered how Satan is able to impact our lives and influence us? How does the devil communicate with us? After all, he is a spirit being, so we cannot hear, see, or touch him, nor can he touch us. I understand how another human being can influence me, because I am a physical being and he is a physical being, as well. Another human being who wants to make an impression on me can do so through his words, which I can hear, or through his actions, which I can see, or through physical touch, which I can feel. How can a spirit being mess with me when he cannot utter words that I can hear or do things that I can see or touch my physical body in a way that I can feel it? How can he influence my life? He influences me through the words that I hear from other people and the words that I say with my own mouth.

Just think about it! Jesus said, *"The words that I speak unto you, they are spirit, and they are life." (John 6:63, KJV)* So, words are *"spirit."* Words have the power to convey from one spiritual being to another spiritual being and from one human's spirit to another human's spirit the things that those two beings want to transfer from themselves to someone else. Satan influences us through words. Though we cannot hear his words because he has no mouth and we do not have the ears that can hear a demonic spirit speaking, he touches our spirits and impacts our minds through the words that we speak to ourselves and the words that others speak to us. Words are powerful things, so we must learn to filter the words that we allow to influence us and filter the words that we say to ourselves and others, especially in times of great testing.

Therefore, King Solomon said, *"Death and life are in the power of the tongue." (Proverbs 18:21, KJV)* Our words either build up or tear down. They either create or destroy. Words are not weightless, even if we don't mean to say them, because whatever comes out of a man's mouth must originate somewhere. It originates with a deeply held belief, whether the person recognizes the presence of that belief in his heart or not. That is why Jesus said, *"The mouth speaks what the heart is full of." (Luke 6:45, NIV)*

You must recognize your entrance into a season of testing by watching the thoughts that flow from your mind and the words that flow from your lips. Your improper thoughts and impure words are sure signs that you have entered a trial. When your words force you to recognize that you are amid a spiritual battle, discipline your tongue while you are there. Give no place to the lies of the devil. Instead, *"in everything give thanks: for this is the will of God in Christ Jesus concerning you." (I Thessalonians 5:18, KJV)* Remember, the words you speak will activate in your life the thing that you are *"saying with"* the devil or *"saying with"* the Lord. The words you speak will unleash either the cruelty of the enemy or the grace of God while you are navigating your ordeal. The choice is yours.

The experiences of Levi, Deborah, and David also show us that there is a third component of a trial. The third sign that we entered testing is the sign of the circumstances that surround us.

Most of the circumstances in our lives are circumstances we cannot control, having nothing to do with our deeds or decisions.

The circumstances that cause us the most sorrow—as well as the most joy—are circumstances we created for ourselves when we planted a *"seed"* that eventually gave birth to the conditions we now must face. If there is deep sorrow in my life because of the circumstances that surround me, those circumstances flow from decisions I made long ago and from the actions I took because of those decisions.

To turn my circumstances around, I must plant new seeds... different kinds of seeds. The good news is that those new seeds will produce a new and different harvest in my life that will choke out the bitter fruit that is sprouting from the seeds I planted in the past. The bad news is the laws of agriculture *(both natural agriculture and spiritual agriculture)* work slowly and take time. So, my new seeds must be planted, germinate, and have time to grow before they can produce their yield. In the meantime, I will have to continue eating the fruits of past choices and actions. This *"in between time"* is what constitutes a trial.

However, the man *(or woman)* who successfully navigates a trial can expect to win in multiple ways despite the pain and suffering. First, he can expect to change his future circumstances by learning from his past mistakes. He can expect to *"grow in grace, and in the knowledge of our Lord and Saviour Jesus Christ." (II Peter 3:18, KJV)* Second, as he sows new seeds in the ground, he can expect a different harvest in the future than the one he has reaped in the past. He can expect his life to take a different direction and produce a different outcome. Third, he can expect to receive the crown of righteousness in Heaven, a crown that is laid up for those who overcome the trials of life and the attacks of the enemy *(see II Timothy 4:8).* Finally, he can expect to enter God's rest, a place that is promised to those who do the right things in the wilderness of testing. God's rest is a place where He can heal the *"spots"* in our souls that contaminated us because our deliverance is complete, and we are able to be restored to our full potential.

God *"delivered"* Levi from the powerful grip of unforgiveness upon his life, God *"delivered"* Deborah from the terrible stain of guilt and shame, and God *"delivered"* David from the self-destructive obsession with being accepted and approved by everyone in his life. Just because a person is *"delivered"* doesn't mean that the person is healed. After he *(or she)* is set free from the control of Satan's devices, that person will be able to enter God's rest, where true healing can occur. So, the person who is amid a struggle with the enemy must rise above the temporary circumstances that oppress him. As he awaits the new and improved circumstances that God has in store for him, he must find that place of total trust and complete confidence in God that yields the rest from his spiritual labor God wants him to enjoy.

How does this observation apply to you? How do the experiences of Levi, Deborah, and David apply to your life and to the struggles you are having in certain areas of godliness? These truths from Scripture apply to you because, like the three people described in this book, you have already been saved by the blood of Jesus and by the word of your testimony. Your spirit is already filled with eternal light. Your soul must be gradually and progressively saved by the implanted Word. Then, you must be healed as God restores you to the person you were created to be. You need to know that the Lord is going to accomplish all this through the process of testing.

So, your trials, though painful for a season, are more important to your spiritual development than God's blessings. Your trials, though difficult and sometimes protracted, are designed to help you apply the Word of God to your life so you can become personally acquainted with Jesus *"and the power of his resurrection, and the fellowship of his sufferings." (Philippians 3:10, KJV)* Your trials are designed to help you break free from the manipulative power of the *"spots"* in your soul as you finally terminate Satan's stranglehold on your life and seize God-given opportunities to become a *"doer"* of the Word and not a *"hearer"* only *(see James 1:22)*.

Thus, the journey from spiritual infancy to maturity is a journey marked with trials. Though you are destined to repeat the trials you fail, God will never give up on you. He will continue to place you in situations that will test your tendency toward unforgiveness, toward shame, and prove or disprove rejection and its accompanying defenses in your life. God will continue to do this until he fully eliminates the residue of deception that Satan currently uses to control you and detract you from the destiny you have as a follower of Jesus Christ. He will allow you to be tested until you overcome what stands in your way through the power of the engrafted Word and enter the spiritual rest the Lord has predestined for you.

In fact, your trials are not a sign that God is displeased with you. On the contrary, they are proof that the Lord has not given up on you. They are evidence that God has endorsed you and He has confidence in you as His child. Your trials—identified by the thoughts they generate, the words they produce, and the circumstances they create—are tools in the hands of the Holy Spirit that He uses to set us free from Satan's control. Although they are weapons in the hands of the enemy, they are weapons that shall not prosper *(see Isaiah 54:17),* because God will take the weapons that Satan uses to destroy us, and He will use them to promote us. Through our trials, the Lord will start unfolding His plan for our lives, a plan that will lead to our inheritance of the promised blessings of His kingdom.

There is a *"seed"* of sin within each of us. In our souls, there is a *"seed"* of the residue of Adam's fall, and that *"seed"* causes us to continually surrender to Satan's deception as we give him unearned control over our lives. When that *"seed"* in our souls is replaced by the incorruptible seed of the Word of God *(see I Peter 1:23)*, the enemy will be forced to yield, even though he will not yield willingly or peaceably. When his domain in our lives is threatened, Satan will come against us with all determination in efforts to retain control over us and fortify his dominance over our thoughts and behaviors through the stain he has nurtured within us. When the light of God's Word begins to expose what Satan is doing so we might be free from his tight-fisted grip, Satan will tempt us and test us, sift us, and pummel us. He will do all that he can do to strengthen his influence rather than surrender it. He will do all that he can do to weaken our resolve rather than yield to it. God will turn his own weaponry upon him as the Lord resurrects our souls to new life and uses what the enemy meant for our harm to accomplish good things on our behalf.

Rest assured that in your times of trial, the adversary will come as *"darkness."* He will try to raise barriers in your mind that obstruct the light of God's Word, reminding you of your prior mistakes and foolish behaviors of the past. In these times, you should always remember that, although your spirit was saved instantaneously at conversion, your soul is being saved gradually as the light of God's Word is absorbed by your mind and applied to your everyday life. The enemy will take advantage of the trials that God allows in your life by using those occasions to raise doubt about the truth of God's word and the accuracy in which it would work for you in your desperate situation.

In addition, when these inevitable times come, and we are forced to walk through that dark valley, we must remember that this is when faith becomes real. When we don't feel like God is working behind the scenes or see His hand at work in our lives, when we don't experience the vindication of God's Word in our circumstances or receive the relief for which we pray, we choose to obey God anyway. We become *"doers of the Word, and not hearers only." (James 1:22, ESV)* Then, these events become the moments when we prevail in our trials. They become the moments when the Word of God turns into something more than just a series of stories about Jesus and the ancient Israelites. These are the moments when God's Word is truly engrafted into our souls as we learn to put it into action and apply it to our circumstances. These are the moments when we are changed.

The enemy won't only manifest as *"darkness"*. He can also appear as *"light"*. He will come as a friend, an advisor, or a compassionate soul who will say things or do things that are designed to get us off course when it comes to the new revelations we are trying to apply to our lives.

Whenever a person takes any initial step of faith toward something new that God is showing to him or demanding from him, that initial step will usually be a little weak and *"wobbly"* because a person must learn to walk before he can run. The apostle Paul is perhaps the best biblical example of this truth, because he spent at least 17 years seeking the Lord and exploring God's call upon his life before he took the step of leaving his home church to establish new congregations throughout the Mediterranean. When Paul finally took this step, Satan resisted him every inch of the way, just as he will resist you when you try to boldly move in a new direction.

During your initial steps of obedience, when you are learning to walk a new path, Satan will oppose you as rigorously as he opposed Paul. While part of his assault on you will be direct, through straightforward opposition, the subtle part of Satan's strategy will be the many *"voices"* he sends your way to pose as messengers of truth and light. They will try to get you to say the wrong words or to do the wrong things, so you will abort what God is trying to *"birth"* in your life as He labors to make His Word a part of your thinking and everyday behavior.

Satan's final weapon of assault against you will be his full-frontal opposition to your growth and success. He will come as darkness and he will come as light, but he will also oppose you through the negative circumstances that he either helps to create around you or uses to his advantage and your detriment.

While we live in this cursed world, we deal with circumstances that are unfavorable to spiritual growth and peace. We deal with people who are a detriment to spiritual growth and peace. Part of the purpose of a trial is to teach us that, while our circumstances may never change, and other people may never change, our attitude about things and our response to them can certainly change. That is when victory comes. When we come to the place where the *"seed"* of residue of Adam's fall no longer governs the way we view the world, God, or ourselves. The troubles surrounding us can no longer manipulate us or control our lives and neither can the wicked people surrounding us. They can no longer get *"inside"* of us. Instead, they will remain external to us and eventually come to serve God's purposes instead of frustrating them.

The journey to God's rest and then to God's promises is one that always passes through some perilous territory. To get from here to there, we must travel through the wilderness of testing. To get from the promise to the provision of that promise, we must pass through some real problems. Only through trials can we come to know the full power and glory of God's presence in our lives, and only through suffering can we find deliverance and healing from the *"spots"* and stains that contaminate our lives. Victory comes as we learn to practically apply God's Word to our individual struggles with unrighteous thinking and the destructive behaviors that follow it.

The prophet Joel proclaimed, *"For he is strong that executeth the word." (Joel 2:11, Webster's Bible Translation)* The ultimate purpose of your trials, therefore, is to help you understand from the Bible those things you have read and learned. Until the Word of God reshapes your thinking, so God can reshape your behavior, you will not grow spiritually or overcome the *"spots"* that took hold of your life when the sin nature within you met the external experiences that shaped you. You will never become *"strong"*.

Your trial is the doorway to that change. It is your pathway from suffering to rest and from rest to the promises of God for your life. Therefore, press in when the enemy is pushing against you. Be determined to *"do"* what you believe. When your mind is renewed by the Word of God and you start executing the precepts of the Lord amid your struggles, Satan will have to release you. Then like our three friends, you will come to experience true freedom and true spiritual growth in a way you never have before.

The apostle John prayed for the early believers that ***"in all respects you may prosper and be in good health, just as your soul prospers." (III John 2, NASB)*** The prosperity of our lives is connected to the prosperity of our souls, and the prosperity of our souls is connected to the prosperity of the Word of God as it is activated through our thinking, feelings, actions, and choices. Every time we allow God's Word and the purifying work of our trials to remove a *"spot"* from our souls, we prosper. We also draw closer to achieving the abundant life God has promised to us as His children. Until the light of God that already shines in our spirits can impact and change our souls, as well, we will not prosper in this life the way that God designed us to prosper. Instead, we will always feel like something is holding us back.

Four Steps To Freedom

The Greek word **euangelion,** *(pronounced you-ang-ghel'-ee-on)* literally means, *"God's good news".* In the New Testament, this word is translated *"gospel".* God's good news *(the gospel)* is the news that God has come in the flesh and paid the penalty for our sins through His death on the cross. It is the news that by the Messiah's death and ensuing resurrection, He now has the authority to deliver us from the power of sin in the same way He has delivered us from the penalty of sin.

Referring to this power of *"deliverance"* would permeate the life and ministry of the coming Messiah, the prophet Isaiah, who lived about 700 years before the birth of Christ, wrote, *"How beautiful on the mountains are the feet of those who bring good news, who proclaim peace, who bring good tidings, who proclaim salvation, who say to Zion, 'Your God reigns!'" (Isaiah 52:7, NIV)*

Isaiah, speaking directly on his own behalf and prophetically on behalf of the coming Savior, also wrote, *"The Spirit of the Sovereign LORD is on me, because the LORD has anointed me to proclaim good news to the poor. He has sent me to bind up the brokenhearted, to proclaim freedom for the captives and release from darkness for the prisoners." (Isaiah 61:1, NIV)*

"Instead of your shame you will receive a double portion, and instead of disgrace you will rejoice in your inheritance. And so, you will inherit a double portion in your land, and everlasting joy will be yours." (Isaiah 61:7, NIV)

Isaiah and the other prophets who spoke about the Messiah wrote about good things to come and the power of the coming Deliverer to heal broken hearts, to liberate imprisoned souls, and to proclaim salvation to all who would be willing to receive it. They wrote welcome news about abundant blessings to follow and the replacement of shame and misfortune with an inheritance that is marked with joy. This was indeed *"good news"* to the people of past generations, and it is *"good news"* to those of us living now who know that there is something more to life than mere survival or just a few years of purposeless existence that is destined to end with death.

The promises of God in the Old Testament, for those of us who have experienced the *"good news"* of the New Testament, is that He has provided for our salvation, for the healing of our broken hearts, and deliverance from both physical and spiritual captivity. He has promised to open the prisons that hold us, remove the shame that binds us, and banish the confusion that encompasses our lives, so we can rejoice in the portion He has bestowed upon us and receive double honor as the heirs of His Kingdom. He has promised, not only to remove the *"spots"*, stains, and blemishes that are blights upon our lives, but to restore what was forfeited because of the presence of these stains in our souls for so long.

In Christ, therefore, we have victory. Because we are His and He abides in us, we have the power to realize all the blessings that God has offered to us through his prophets, and we have the potential of attaining all the promises God has made available to us through his Word. In Christ, the *"good news"* is that we can be free in every way and accomplish everything with our lives that

God gave us the potential to accomplish when He formed us in our mother's wombs.

As it is with all of God's promises, we must do something to activate them. We must do something to appropriate them in our lives. In fact, we must do more than just believe God's promises; we must act upon the promises that God has made to us if we ever hope to realize the full benefit of his *"good news"*. The way we act upon God's promises is by obeying the conditions that accompany them.

Just think about it! It is not enough for a person to simply believe that God exists. It is not enough for a person to believe that the Bible is true. *"You say you have faith, for you believe that there is one God. Good for you!"* James told the early believers. ***"Even the demons believe this, and they tremble in terror."*** *(**James 2:19, NLT**)* Mental belief by itself is not sufficient to change our lives. When we dare to *"submit ourselves to God"* and *"resist the devil,"* the power of the Gospel is activated in our lives and the devil flees from us in defeat *(see James 4:7).* Therefore, faith demonstrated and activated by obedient action is the pathway to deliverance from our bonds.

The writer of Hebrews could truthfully say, ***"For we (the believers) also have had the good news proclaimed to us, just as they (the unbelievers) did; but the message they heard was of no value to them, because they did not share the faith of those who obeyed it."*** *(Hebrews 4:2, NIV)* Simply *"hearing"* the Word of God isn't enough to activate the promises of God in our lives. Simply *"hearing"* the *"good news"* isn't enough for obtaining salvation, for procuring our deliverance. To see God's promises fulfilled in our lives, we need to act upon what we have heard. We need to do something in response to God's Word as it impacts our minds and our hearts. We must *"believe and obey"* rather than *"believe and tremble"* as the demons do, because real faith combines with the Word of God through obedience, thus producing a *"new creature"* in every possible aspect of that phrase. When we *"believe and obey"* as the Bible encourages us to do, we receive ***"the outcome of (our) faith, the salvation of (our) souls." (I Peter 1:9, ESV)*** By receiving and believing the Word—by combining God's Word with our faith—we experience the removal of Satan's *"spots"* from our souls, and we are made whole in every way. We experience the *"outcome of our faith"* and the complete redemption of our souls because God's power, manifested through His Word, sends the evil spirits in our lives packing *(see Matthew 12:28).*

Satan is strong; there is no doubt about it. He is also highly experienced at destroying the lives of God's people. ***"When one stronger than he attacks him and overcomes him, he takes away his armor in which he trusted and divides his spoil" (Luke 11:22, ESV),*** because God works through our faith to appropriate His will in our lives. We learn to do more than simply listen to the Word. When we grasp the importance and the urgency of obeying God after we hear him speak to us, the Lord strips Satan from the armor in which he trusted, and divides the *"spoils"* so that we become ***"more than conquerors through him who loved us" (Romans 8:37, NIV)*** and ***"If the Son sets you free, you really will be free." (John 8:36, Holman)***

If you are a Christian, you can *"bind"* and *"loose"* the strongman all day long. It's not catchphrases or empty slogans that will chase away the enemy and loosen the shackles that constrain you; it's the truth that will set you free. It's a personal encounter with the truth that will bring you to a life-changing realization of what is deficient within your soul and what God wants you to do about your deficiency, so He can release you to be everything He created you to be. The *"light"* already present in your spirit through faith must impact your intellect, your will, your emotions, and your affections. God can set you on a path you have never traveled, a path that leads to more godly behaviors and a greater outcome for your life.

Let God change your life. Let him take you to places you have never been in your Christian walk and let Him help you achieve your assigned destiny in Christ. Give the Lord permission to drive the enemy from his *"place"* in your soul by making up your mind that you will do these four things to move your spiritual life forward and thus change the direction and outcome of your life:

1. Identify Your Spot By Its Defenses

The *"spots"* Satan creates in our lives are spots that are *"unknown,"* *"hidden,"* and *"blind."* We won't be able to recognize them in our own lives without the help of the Holy Spirit. Where there is fire, there is smoke. Where there are discernible patterns of Satanic *"defenses,"* rest assured there will be a noticeable *"spot"* somewhere behind those fiery darts. If you can identify the *"defenses"*, you can identify the *"spot"*.

Have you ever watched one of those old Westerns on television, particularly one of the old black-and-white Westerns from the late 1950's and early '60's? In almost every one of those old shows, there would be a gunfight at the end of the program. There would be a shootout between the good guys and the bad guys. While every one of these shows ended with both sides digging in for a protracted gunfight, the scene would almost always conclude with the bad guys coming out from behind their protective covering and being shot by Matt Dillon or The Lone Ranger. The same was true in the old military movies about battles during World War II. In those old movies, the Germans would always come out from behind their protection, and, in clear view of the Americans, be shot down and killed.

I used to wonder why the bad guys, who were securely entrenched behind barn doors and rock formations, would come out from behind those protective barriers, exposing themselves to Wyatt Earp's deadly fire or Roy Roger's failproof marksmanship. While these scenarios were the result of the innocent imagination of early television writers, this same scenario is a matter of reality for the Christian who appropriates the Word of God in his life.

The light of God's Word will drive the enemy into the open. It will expose his sinister schemes as God exposes the genuine, unvarnished nature of our souls. Whenever we approach a threshold of change that God has ordained for our lives or we dare to ascend to a higher plane of spiritual maturity, the enemy will always show his hand. In a desperate effort to cling to his foothold in our lives, the devil will no longer hide behind cleverly constructed walls of deceit he has erected over time. Instead, he will openly flaunt the *"defenses"* he has put in place to safeguard his grip on our souls. This desperate move will clearly expose both his presence in our lives and his intentions toward us.

For instance, if a person has been harboring unforgiveness in his heart, even subconsciously, it will become obvious to others as they see the anger and the envy erupt from this person's soul. As the man himself notices increasing displays of jealousy, bitterness, pride, or complaining flow from his life, that will serve as his wake-up call that something is wrong in his soul and that God is touching that *"spot"* which needs to be healed, that part of his life that needs to be restored. As explained in the previous chapter, this will occur in the context of a trial. In the fires and the storms of life, God gives us our deepest and clearest glimpses into the makeup of our own souls.

The *"spots"* that are described in this book are the *"high places"* that Paul describes as eventually being *"cast down"* when we learn to take control of our own thoughts and bring our imaginations into submission to the authority of Christ *(see II Corinthians 10:5)*. Until our thoughts are subdued, and our vain imaginations are conquered, these *"high places"* will continue to rule over us. They will become the places at which we *"worship"* ourselves by turning a blind eye to our own destructive behaviors and make excuses for ourselves rather than accepting responsibility for our shortcomings. They will become the *"trash cans"* into which we dump all our emotional baggage, hoping that it will somehow go away and stop stinking up our lives.

Jesus is the one who can take away our invisible *"garbage"*. He is the one who can clean up our lives. He does this through our obedience, which makes us willing participants in our own rescue. Jesus will do the work, but we must let him do the work, and we must cooperate with him while he is doing the work. We must allow him to use testing to sift us, break us, and expose what is truly inside of us. Then, as we become aware of the true nature of our own souls because of the *"defenses"* we raise to excuse ourselves from righteous living, we come to understand what is deficient within our own hearts and what God needs to do to liberate us from Satan's control.

Until a doctor can diagnose a person's physical problem, that person won't know what to do to alleviate the pain that is ruining his life. Until we know the true nature of our own souls, we won't know what to do to appropriate biblical truth in our lives. The *"defenses"* we manifest when trials beset us will show the nature of the *"spots"* that contaminate us and the *"high places"* that dominate our lives. Once we know the nature of the problem, we will know what God wants us to do to purge that *"infection"* from our lives.

2. Submit To The Truth of Christ

Someone once told me something about adversity that gave me a very different perspective about suffering. This person told me, whenever someone rebukes me for something in my life, my first reaction should always be to seriously weigh the rebuke I receive. *"If the rebuke proves to be true and appropriate,"* the person said, *"then you will be a better person by paying attention to that rebuke and by responding to it through repentance. If the rebuke proves to be untrue or inappropriate, you will still be a better person because the rebuke will give you an opportunity to know your own heart better and to make sure that your life is right with God."*

I thought about this for a while and realized that my friend had given me some wise counsel because this is the attitude all Christians should exhibit whenever they encounter an unpleasant experience in life. Whether we are talking about a confrontation with another person or a protracted journey through a difficult trial, it is always the unpleasant experiences of life that give us opportunities to grow. Unfortunately, most of us don't take advantage of these opportunities. We don't seize those occasions to search our own hearts or weigh our own lives in the balance of practical analysis. Instead we squander those precious opportunities, and we let them make us bitter instead of better as we desperately seek to escape from them.

Nevertheless, they will keep coming. Jesus promised us in no uncertain terms that **"here on earth you will have many trials and sorrows." (John 16:33, NLT)** We must take advantage of trials when they come by extracting all the benefits they were designed to provide. One of the most important benefits we can derive from a trial is to notice the kinds of things that are flowing out in the face of that trial, so we can know what kind of *"spot"* or stain may be contaminating our souls. Trials are God's primary tool for showing us that we need to start resisting the devil in an area of our lives, so he will flee from us as he fled from Jesus in the wilderness *(compare Matthew 4:11 and James 4:7).*

Before you knew how all this works, you probably responded to the trials in your life by subconsciously manifesting one or more of the *"defenses"* Satan fashioned within your soul to protect the *"spot"* he nurtured there. In fact, you grew so accustomed over the years to responding to difficulty the same way every time, you came to take your reactions for granted. *"Oh, that's just the way I am,"* you would say. *"That anger is just the Irish in me... or the Italian... or whatever." "I don't think I'm all that jealous. That's just my personality. Besides, I have every right to be jealous. I've been hurt so many times."*

From now on—since you now know the truth—God is going to use your trials to open your eyes to the presence of a particular *"spot"* in your soul, and you are going to suddenly find yourself standing at a crossroads where you have never stood before. You are going to find yourself at a place where you must make a choice. For the first time, you will have the power to choose between life and death. You will have the power to choose between Satan and the Word of God because you will know what is going on in the spirit realm. My hope is that you will have the power to resist your old, familiar patterns of behavior and instead to choose a new path for yourself as you *"crucify the flesh with its passions and desires." (Galatians 5:24, NASB)*

When Satan's defenses are triggered, particularly during a trial, refuse to yield to them as you have yielded in the past. Instead, stand still, confess the Word of God in faith, and see the salvation God accomplishes in your soul through Jesus Christ. Don't think that you only need to resist the devil once to win this war. You must resist him over and over again. Remember, when Jesus refused to turn the stones into bread when Satan tempted him in the wilderness, the devil came back a second time and tempted Jesus to jump off the pinnacle of the temple. When Jesus resisted the devil's temptation to prove His divinity by jumping from the top of the temple, the devil came back one more time to entice Jesus to worship him in exchange for the kingdoms of the world.

Satan won't give up easily or quickly. If we continually resist him after discovering his ploy in our lives, he will eventually back down. In the same way he finally left Jesus in the wilderness, he will leave us. Then, the angels of God will come to minister to our needs the same way they came to minister to Christ following his successful resistance from the devil *(see Matthew 4:1-11)*.

3. Experience Restoration

Everything God does, He does with a redemptive purpose in mind. Even God's judgments are designed to redeem. When God touches our lives, through the trials that we endure, He does so to heal us, restore us, and set us on a path to wholeness in every dimension of our lives.

When your struggles become difficult, your trials become unbearable, your enemies become many, when you are forced to confront life's inevitable moments of despair and doubt, remember this powerful certainty that finds its roots in the Bible: God is on your side. He is never *against* you. He is always *for* you.

"For I know the plans I have for you, plans to prosper you and not to harm you, plans to give you hope and a future." (Jeremiah 29:11, NIV)

"Is anything too hard for me?" the Lord asks." (Jeremiah 32:27, NIV)

"I will restore you to health and heal your wounds; declares the LORD." (Jeremiah 30:17, NIV)

"I will fulfill the good promise I made." (Jeremiah 33:14, NIV)

Be patient and trust the Lord as He exposes your weaknesses and deficiencies. When the trials of life start making your faults obvious to you and to others, just remember that God is bringing those things to light, not because He is angry with you, but because He wants to heal them and restore you to your full potential in Him. God can't heal you until He first deals with the source of your problem like the way than a doctor can't heal you without dealing with the source of your pain.

The Lord's main goal in your life, therefore, is to work in you until you are *"perfect and complete, lacking nothing." (James 1:4, NIV)* It is never his objective to condemn or embarrass you. It is never His desire to destroy you or to hurt you in any way. A doctor might *"wound"* you surgically to heal you physically. In the same way God *"wounded"* Jacob by displacing his hip so that things could be made right in Jacob's life, God may *"wound"* you from time to time to make some things right with you and heal things that need His touch. God's ultimate objective is to bring you to complete spiritual health, maturity, and to make you stronger by eliminating those thoughts, feelings, and attitudes from your life that lead you to do things that are contrary to His will and detrimental to your own wellbeing. His objective is never to punish you.

Always remember that suffering—the suffering that purifies our hearts and builds our faith—typically attracts a lot of *"fixers."* When people see us suffering in ways they deem unacceptable, they tend to act like Job's friends surrounding us, not to encourage us or comfort us in the battle, but rather so they can *"fix"* whatever they perceive to be wrong in our lives. My advice to you as one who has *"been there, done that"* is to shun most of the superficial advice you get during these difficult times. Instead, just be patient and let God be God in your life. He has a plan for you, and His plan is specifically designed to take you through troubled waters from time to time. Those waters are meant to heal not kill, to build not destroy, to restore not condemn.

Satan is the one who will try to help you cut your suffering short, because he doesn't want you to grow, and he wants to preserve his foothold in your life. God is the one who knows exactly what you need to overcome your limitations, and God is the One who knows exactly how much of your trial you can endure. Let the Lord have His way with you. Then, watch as He liberates you from your chains and restores you, as He did with Job, to a place of double honor.

4. Live The Abundant Life of Christ

Real faith is refined in the fires and storms of life. Therefore, worship God through your trials, just as Job worshipped God through his trials. Do not succumb to your natural instincts or go to extremes to avoid suffering or lessen your suffering when you are to endure it. Instead, let your suffering take you to new depths in Christ.

Obviously, you don't want to become a masochist. You don't want to start looking for ways to suffer so you can become more spiritual, and you don't want to start wearing your suffering on your sleeve, so it becomes a badge of honor when you are around other Christians. When you do suffer for the sake of Christ, allow the Holy Spirit to do His perfecting work in you. If you do, *"the Spirit of glory and of God rests on you." (I Peter 4:14, NIV)* When you're suffering is finally concluded, you will be free from your bonds and the stains that have contaminated your soul for so long. You will be *"without spot or wrinkle or any such thing." (Ephesians 5:27, ESV)* You will know firsthand the promised rest of God for your soul.

God gives us victory through our Lord Jesus Christ. He gives us victory so we can showcase His glory by living the abundant life that He promised to those who love Him. When we overcome the power of the devil and the negative influences of life's challenges, we are changed in positive ways due to the good fight we have fought. We will enter the blessings of God and the people around us will see that we are different and that our lives are rich in every way. When people start noticing these things in our lives, God will be glorified, and His kingdom will be positively represented to the skeptics around us.

If you have ever been a salesman, then you know that the essence of good salesmanship is found in the ability to showcase one's product or service. To showcase a product in a convincing manner, a good salesman must be able to communicate all the benefits a person can derive by using the salesman's product.

The godly life, like a salesman's product, has benefits that can enrich a person's life. God communicates these benefits for us in the Bible. Through His messenger, King David, God tells us to *"Bless the LORD, O my soul, and forget not all his benefits." (Psalm 103:2, NKJV)*

What are the *"benefits"* of serving God? What are the *"benefits"* of the abundant life that you can expect to derive from your intimacy with the Lord? Not only will rivers of living water flow from your inner being *(see John 7:38)* and not only will you live your life with the knowledge that you will dwell in God's presence forever *(see Psalm 23:6)*, but God also will:

1. Forgive all your iniquity *(Psalm 103:3)*
2. Heal all your diseases *(Psalm 103:3)*
3. Redeem your life from the pit *(Psalm 103:4)*
4. Crown you with steadfast love and mercy *(Psalm 103:4)*
5. Satisfy you with good as long as you live *(Psalm 103:5)*
6. Renew your youth like the eagle's *(Psalm 103:5)*

God wants us to *"know him, and the power of his resur-rection, and the fellowship of his sufferings" (Philippians 3:10, KJV)* so we can live the blessed and abundant life that will showcase His glory and call attention to His splendor, thus attracting to Him all the people in this world who have an inaccurate understanding of who He really is.

God doesn't want you to wait for heaven to experience the fullness of His kingdom and inherit His rewards. He doesn't want you to wait for heaven to reap the benefits of a righteous life or the advantages of a faithful heart. God wants you to know the fullness of His riches and the fullness of His power right now, today, and from this day forward.

Let the Lord change you. Let Him set you free from all that is holding you back in your pursuit of Him and your efforts to walk as a citizen of His kingdom. The Lord will never be content to leave you in your current state because you belong to Him and not to Satan. He will never be content to leave you in your present bondage. God has something better for you. The rest of your life can be the best of your life.

You must know what God is doing so you can participate in your own rescue. You must let God help you overcome the one who is interfering with the rich and wonderful destiny that God has already written for your life. When you do allow God to set you free from the prison you have occupied far too long, you will be well on your way to God's perfect plan for your life and God will be able to use you in ways you have never known before. You will finally be *"free indeed" (John 8:36, NIV).*

Scripture References

The following scriptural passages are those that are quoted within the text of the book or referenced as applicable to the book's overall message. These passages are referenced in order of the books of the Bible, and the versions noted are those that are utilized in the text of the book.

Proverbs 28:26 (NKJV) *"Those who trust in themselves are fools, but those who walk in wisdom are kept safe."*

Genesis 3:10 (NIV) *(Adam) answered, "I heard you in the garden, and I was afraid because I was naked; so I hid."*

Deuteronomy 31:6 (NLT) *"So be strong and courageous! Do not be afraid and do not panic before them. For the LORD your God will personally go ahead of you. He will neither fail you nor abandon you."*

Psalm 23:4 (KJV) *"Yea, though I walk through the valley of the shadow of death, I will fear no evil: for thou art with me; thy rod and thy staff they comfort me."*

Psalm 23:6 (KJV) *"Surely goodness and mercy shall follow me all the days of my life: and I will dwell in the house of the LORD forever."*

Psalm 103:2-5 (RSV) *"Bless the LORD, O my soul, and forget not all his benefits, who forgives all your iniquity, who heals all your diseases, who redeems your life from the Pit, who crowns you with steadfast love and mercy, who satisfies you with good as long as you live so that your youth is renewed like the eagle's."*

Psalm 119:105 (KJV) *"Thy word is a lamp unto my feet, and a light unto my path."*

Psalm 139:23 (KJV) *"Search me, O God, and know my heart: try me, and know my thoughts."*

Proverbs 18:21 (KJV) *"Death and life are in the power of the tongue: and they that love it shall eat the fruit thereof."*

Proverbs 19:2 (NIV) *"Desire without knowledge is not good— how much more will hasty feet miss the way!"*

Proverbs 23:7 (KJV) *"For as he thinketh in his heart, so is he."*

Proverbs 28:13 (NLT) "People who conceal their sins will not prosper, but if they confess and turn from them, they will receive mercy."

Proverbs 29:18 (KJV) *"Where there is no vision, the people perish: but he that keepeth the law, happy is he."*

Isaiah 52:7 (NIV) *"How beautiful on the mountains are the feet of those who bring good news, who proclaim peace, who bring good tidings, who proclaim salvation, who say to Zion, Your God reigns!"*

Isaiah 53:3 (NLT) *"He was despised and rejected—a man of sorrows, acquainted with deepest grief. We turned our backs on him and looked the other way. He was despised, and we did not care."*

Isaiah 54:17 (NASB) *"No weapon that is formed against you will prosper; and every tongue that accuses you in judgment you will condemn. This is the heritage of the servants of the LORD, and their vindication is from Me," declares the LORD.*

Isaiah 61:1 (NIV) *"The Spirit of the Sovereign LORD is on me, because the LORD has anointed me to proclaim good news to the poor. He has sent me to bind up the brokenhearted, to proclaim freedom for the captives and release from darkness for the prisoners...."*

Isaiah 61:7 (NIV) *"Instead of your shame you will receive a double portion, and instead of disgrace you will rejoice in your inheritance. And so you will inherit a double portion in your land, and everlasting joy will be yours."*

Jeremiah 29:11 (NIV) *"For I know the plans I have for you," declares the LORD, "plans to prosper you and not to harm you, plans to give you hope and a future."*

Jeremiah 30:17 (NIV) *"But I will restore you to health and heal your wounds," declares the LORD, "because you are called an outcast, Zion for whom no one cares."*

Jeremiah 32:27 (NIV) *"I am the LORD, the God of all mankind. Is anything too hard for me?"*

Jeremiah 33:14 (NIV) *"The days are coming," declares the LORD, "when I will fulfill the good promise I made to the people of Israel and Judah."*

Joel 2:11 (Webster's Bible Translation) *"And the LORD will utter his voice before his army: for his camp is very great: for he is strong that executeth his word: for the day of the LORD is great and very terrible; and who can abide it?"*

Matthew 4:11 (NIV) *"Then the devil left him, and angels came and attended him."*

Matthew 6:15 (NLT) *"But if you refuse to forgive others, your Father will not forgive your sins."*

Matthew 7:16 (NIV) *"By their fruit you will recognize them. Do people pick grapes from thornbushes, or figs from thistles?"*

Matthew 11:12 (ESV) *"From the days of John the Baptist until now the kingdom of heaven has suffered violence, and the violent take it by force."*

Matthew 12:28 (NLT) *"But if I am casting out demons by the Spirit of God, then the Kingdom of God has arrived among you."*

Matthew 12:34 (ESV) *"You brood of vipers! How can you speak good, when you are evil? For out of the abundance of the heart the mouth speaks."*

Matthew 16:18 (KJV) *"And I say also unto thee, that thou art Peter, and upon this rock I will build my church; and the gates of hell shall not prevail against it."*

Mark 16:17 (KJV) *"And these signs shall follow them that believe; in my name shall they cast out devils; they shall speak with new tongues."*

Luke 6:45 (ESV) *"The good person out of the good treasure of his heart produces good, and the evil person out of his evil treasure produces evil, for out of the abundance of the heart his mouth speaks."*

Luke 11:21-22 (NIV) *"When a strong man, fully armed, guards his own house, his possessions are safe. But when someone stronger attacks and overpowers him, he takes away the armor in which the man trusted and divides up his plunder."*

John 6:63 (KJV) *"It is the spirit that quickeneth; the flesh profiteth nothing: the words that I speak unto you, they are spirit, and they are life."*

John 7:38 (KJV) *"He that believeth on me, as the scripture hath said, out of his belly shall flow rivers of living water."*

John 8:36 (NIV) *"Therefore, if the Son sets you free, you really will be free."*

John 10:10 (KJV) *"The thief cometh not, but for to steal, and to kill, and to destroy: I am come that they might have life, and that they might have it more abundantly."*

John 15:8 (ESV) *"By this my Father is glorified, that you bear much fruit and so prove to be my disciples."*

John 16:33 (NLT) *"I have told you all this so that you may have peace in me. Here on earth you will have many trials and sorrows. But take heart, because I have overcome the world."*

Romans 5:8 (ESV) *"But God shows his love for us in that while we were still sinners, Christ died for us."*

Romans 8:11 (NIV) *"And if the Spirit of him who raised Jesus from the dead is living in you, he who raised Christ from the dead will also give life to your mortal bodies because of his Spirit who lives in you."*

Romans 8:37 (NIV) *"No, in all these things we are more than conquerors through him who loved us."*

Romans 12:2-3 (NIV) *"Do not conform to the pattern of this world, but be transformed by the renewing of your mind. Then you will be able to test and approve what God's will is—his good, pleasing and perfect will. For by the grace given me I say to every one of you: Do not think of yourself more highly than you ought, but rather think of yourself with sober judgment, in accordance with the faith God has distributed to each of you."*

II Corinthians 3:18 (KJV) *"But we all, with open face beholding as in a glass the glory of the Lord, are changed into the same image from glory to glory, even as by the Spirit of the Lord."*

II Corinthians 10:4-6 (NIV) *"The weapons we fight with are not the weapons of the world. On the contrary, they give divine power to demolish strongholds. We demolish arguments and every pretension that sets itself up against the knowledge of God, and we take captive every thought to make it obedient to Christ. And we will be ready to punish every act of disobedience, once your obedience is complete."*

Galatians 3:14 (NIV) *"He redeemed us in order that the blessing given to Abraham might come to the Gentiles through Christ Jesus, so that by faith we might receive the promise of the Spirit."*

Galatians 4:2 (NIV) *"The heir is subject to guardians and trustees until the time set by his father."*

Galatians 5:9 (ESV) *"A little leaven leavens the whole lump."*

Galatians 5:24 (NASB) *"Now those who belong to Christ Jesus have crucified the flesh with its passions and desires."*

Ephesians 1:3-8 (NIV) *"Praise be to the God and Father of our Lord Jesus Christ, who has blessed us in the heavenly realms with every spiritual blessing in Christ. For he chose us in him before the creation of the world to be holy and blameless in his sight. In love he predestined us for adoption to sonship through Jesus Christ, in accordance with his pleasure and will—to the praise of his glorious grace, which he has freely given us in the One he loves. In him we have redemption through his blood, the forgiveness of sins, in accordance with the riches of God's grace that he lavished on us."*

Ephesians 4:11-14 (NIV) *"So Christ himself gave the apostles, the prophets, the evangelists, the pastors and teachers, to equip his people for works of service, so that the body of Christ may be built up until we all reach unity in the faith and in the knowledge of the Son of God and become mature, attaining to the whole measure of the fullness of Christ. Then we will no longer be infants, tossed back and forth by the waves, and* *blown here and there by every wind of teaching and by the cunning and craftiness of people in their deceitful scheming."*

Ephesians 4:22-24 (KJV) *"That ye put off concerning the former conversation the old man, which is corrupt according to the deceitful lusts; and be renewed in the spirit of your mind; and that ye put on the new man, which after God is created in righteousness and true holiness."*

Ephesians 4:27 (KJV) *"Neither give place to the devil."*

Ephesians 5:25-27 (KJV) *"Husbands, love your wives, even as Christ also loved the church, and gave himself for it; that he might sanctify and cleanse it with the washing of water by the word, that he might present it to himself a glorious church, not having spot, or wrinkle, or any such thing; but that it should be holy and without blemish."*

Ephesians 6:16 (KJV) *"Above all, taking the shield of faith, wherewith ye shall be able to quench all the fiery darts of the wicked."*

Philippians 2:12 (NIV) *"Therefore, my dear friends, as you have always obeyed—not only in my presence, but now much more in my absence—continue to work out your salvation with fear and trembling...."*

Philippians 3:10 (KJV) *"That I may know him, and the power of his resurrection, and the fellowship of his sufferings, being made conformable unto his death."*

I Thessalonians 5:18 (KJV) *"In every thing give thanks: for this is the will of God in Christ Jesus concerning you."*

II Timothy 4:8 (NIV) *"Now there is in store for me the crown of righteousness, which the Lord, the righteous Judge, will award to me on that day—and not only to me, but also to all who have longed for his appearing."*

Hebrews 4:2-3 (NIV) *"For we also have had the good news proclaimed to us, just as they did; but the message they heard was of no value to them, because they did not share the faith of those who obeyed. Now we who have believed enter that rest, just as God has said, "So I declared on oath in my anger, 'They shall never enter my rest.'" And yet his works have been finished since the creation of the world."*

Hebrews 4:12-13 (NLT) *"For the word of God is alive and powerful. It is sharper than the sharpest two-edged sword, cutting between soul and spirit, between joint and marrow. It exposes our innermost thoughts and desires. Nothing in all creation is hidden from God. Everything is naked and exposed before his eyes, and he is the one to whom we are accountable."*

Hebrews 6:1-2 (NIV) *"Therefore let us move beyond the elementary teachings about Christ and be taken forward to maturity, not laying again the foundation of repentance from acts that lead to death and of faith in God, instruction about cleansing rites, the laying on of hands, the resurrection of the dead, and eternal judgment."*

Hebrews 12:2 (NLT) *"We do this by keeping our eyes on Jesus, the champion who initiates and perfects our faith. Because of the joy awaiting him, he endured the cross, disregarding its shame. Now he is seated in the place of honor beside God's throne."*

Hebrews 12:15 (NLT) *"Look after each other so that none of you fails to receive the grace of God. Watch out that no poisonous root of bitterness grows up to trouble you, corrupting many."*

James 1:4 (NIV) *"Let perseverance finish its work so that you may be mature and complete, not lacking anything."*

James 1:6 (KJV) *"But let him ask in faith, nothing wavering. For he that wavereth is like a wave of the sea driven with the wind and tossed."*

James 1:22 (ESV) *"But be doers of the word, and not hearers only, deceiving yourselves."*

James 1:27 (KJV) *"Pure religion and undefiled before God and the Father is this, to visit the fatherless and widows in their affliction, and to keep himself unspotted from the world."*

James 2:19 (NLT) *"You say you have faith, for you believe that there is one God. Good for you! Even the demons believe this, and they tremble in terror."*

James 4:7 (KJV) *"Submit yourselves therefore to God. Resist the devil, and he will flee from you."*

I Peter 1:8-9 (ESV) *"Though you have not seen him, you love him. Though you do not now see him, you believe in him and rejoice with joy that is inexpressible and filled with glory, obtaining the outcome of your faith, the salvation of your souls."*

I Peter 1:23 (NIV) *"For you have been born again, not of perishable seed, but of imperishable, through the living and enduring word of God."*

I Peter 4:14 (NIV) *"If you are insulted because of the name of Christ, you are blessed, for the Spirit of glory and of God rests on you."*

I Peter 5:10 (NASB) *"After you have suffered for a little while, the God of all grace, who called you to His eternal glory in Christ, will Himself perfect, confirm, strengthen and establish you."*

II Peter 1:3-4 (NIV) *"His divine power has given us everything we need for a godly life through our knowledge of him who called us by his own glory and goodness. Through these he has given us his very great and precious promises, so that through them you may participate in the divine nature, having escaped the corruption in the world caused by evil desires."*

II Peter 2:13 (NIV) *"They will be paid back with harm for the harm they have done. Their idea of pleasure is to carouse in broad daylight. They are blots and blemishes, reveling in their pleasures while they feast with you."*

II Peter 3:18 (KJV) *"But grow in grace, and in the knowledge of our Lord and Saviour Jesus Christ. To him be glory both now and for ever. Amen."*

I John 1:6-7 (NIV) *"If we claim to have fellowship with him and yet walk in the darkness, we lie and do not live out the truth. But if we walk in the light, as he is in the light, we have fellowship with one another, and the blood of Jesus, his Son, purifies us from all sin."*

I John 2:8 (NIV) *"Yet I am writing you a new command; its truth is seen in him and in you, because the darkness is passing and the true light is already shining."*

III John 2 (NASB) *"Beloved I pray that in all respects you may prosper and be in good health, just as your soul prospers."*

Jude 11-12 (ESV) *"Woe to them! For they walked in the way of Cain and abandoned themselves for the sake of gain to Balaam's error and perished in Korah's rebellion. These are hidden reefs at your love feasts, as they feast with you without fear, shepherds feeding themselves; waterless clouds, swept along by winds; fruitless trees in late autumn, twice dead, uprooted...."*

Jude 16 (NIV) *"These people are grumblers and faultfinders; they follow their own evil desires; they boast about themselves and flatter others for their own advantage."*

Revelation 2:7, 11, 17, 26 (KJV) *"He that hath an ear, let him hear what the Spirit saith unto the churches; to him that overcometh will I give to eat of the tree of life, which is in the midst of the paradise of God.... He that overcometh shall not be hurt of the second death.... To him that overcometh will I give to eat of the hidden manna, and will give him a white stone, and in the stone a new name written, which no man knoweth saving he that receiveth it.... And he that overcometh, and keepeth my works unto the end, to him will I give power over the nations."*

Revelation 3:5, 12, 21 (KJV) *"He that overcometh, the same shall be clothed in white raiment; and I will not blot out his name out of the book of life, but I will confess his name before my Father, and before his angels.... Him that overcometh will I make a pillar in the temple of my God, and he shall go no more out: and I will write upon him the name of my God, and the name of the city of my God, which is new Jerusalem, which cometh down out of heaven from my God: and I will write upon him my new name.... To him that overcometh will I grant to sit with me in my throne, even as I also overcame, and am set down with my Father in his throne."*

Revelation 12:11 (KJV) *"And they overcame him by the blood of the Lamb, and by the word of their testimony; and they loved not their lives unto the death."*

Revelation 19:7 (NIV) *"Let us rejoice and be glad and give him glory! For the wedding of the Lamb has come, and his bride has made herself ready."*

SELA - Lewis Cancer Pavillion
225 Candler Dr Suite 301 Savannah, GA 31405-6091
Phone: (912) 819-5757 , Fax: (912) 228-8242

Edith Utley PA
DEA: MU1744639
NPI: 1003951658

Date: 9/9/2019

Name: JUDY NEASE
DOB: 01/14/1938   Age: 81 years
Gender: Female
Phone: (912) 897-2485
Address: 924 WILMINGTON ISLAND ROAD, SAVANNAH, GA   31410

Pharmacy:
Address: ,
Phone:
Fax:

RX.

SELA - Lewis Cancer Pavillion
225 Candler Dr Suite 301 Savannah, GA 31405-6091
Phone: (912) 819-5757 , Fax: (912) 228-8242

Edith Utley PA
DEA: MU1744639
NPI: 1003951658

Date: 9/9/2019

Name: JUDY NEASE
DOB: 01/14/1938   Age: 81 years
Gender: Female
Phone: (912) 897-2485
Address: 924 WILMINGTON ISLAND ROAD, SAVANNAH, GA 31410

Pharmacy:
Address: ,
Phone:
Fax:

RX:

SIG: Take 1 tablet by mouth daily
Refill(s): None x None
Comments: Use in comination with 5mg ~~1mg~~ tabs to wean prednisone by 1mg per week.

Associated Diagnosis
* ILD (515 | J84.9)

Substitution Permissible
Prescription is medically necessary

Start with 9mg daily x 7days
then
8mg daily x 7days,
7mg daily x 7days,
6mg daily x 7 days,
5mg daily x 7 days,
4mg daily x 7 days,
3mg daily x 7days,
2mg daily x 7 days,
1mg daily x 7 days
stop.

Edith Utley PA-C

Electronically signed on 9/9/2019
Edith Utley PA
NPI: 1003951658
DEA: MU1744639
License: 004777, GA

SIG: 1 (one) Tablet by mouth as directed
Refill(s): None x None
Comments: Use in combination with 5mg tabs to decrease by 1 mg weekly

Associated Diagnosis
* ILD (515 | J84.9)

Substitution Permissible
Prescription is medically necessary

see other Rx
for instructions

Edith Utley PA-C

Electronically signed on 9/9/2019
Edith Utley PA
NPI: 1003951658
DEA: MU1744639
License: 004777, GA

255602

3932
$10382

11477 66

Judy Nease